DEDICATION

To Evangeline and Julian, my very favorite sewing-space buddies and agents of chaos.

ACKNOWLEDGMENTS

First and foremost, I owe enormous thanks to my family: To my daughter, Evie, who helped with several quilts by tearing away piecing papers and by helping glue baste (even though she tried to use a whole glue stick on each piece), and to my son, Julian, who helps keep my work surfaces clear by removing anything within reach (and, by corollary, training me to keep my rotary cutters locked and put away). And, of course, to my husband, Adrian, who tolerates the chaos in and out of the quilting studio.

I could not find the perfect quilting design for three of the quilts in this book, so I am deeply grateful to Barbie Mills of The Quilting Mill for designing digital pantographs especially for them. I am also grateful to Sheila Shepherd of Thirty4Stitches for longarming them for me and taking extra care to make sure that the quilting was just right.

Thanks to Wade Sheldon for lending me tripods, giving photo advice, and, most importantly, for taking the glamour shots in this book (under extreme time-crunch conditions!) to show my quilts in their very best light.

Finally, I am thankful to the entire C&T crew, and especially to my editor, Roxane Cerda, for helping this vision become reality and answering my endless questions along the way.

Contents

Modern Scrap QUILTS

Playing with Negative Space

SYLVIA SCHAEFER

Publisher: Amy Barrett-Daffin

Creative Director: Gailen Runge

Senior Editor: Roxane Cerda

Technical Editor: Sarah Ruiz

Copy Editor: Second Glance Editorial

Cover/Book Designer: April Mostek

Production Coordinator: Tim Manibusan

Illustrator: Kirstie Pettersen

Photography Coordinator: Rachel Ackley

Front cover photography by Wade Sheldon Photography

Subjects photography by C&T Publishing, Inc.; lifestyle photography by Wade Sheldon Photography; instructional photography by Sylvia Schaefer, unless otherwise noted

Published by Stash Books, an imprint of C&T Publishing, Inc., P.O. Box 1456, Lafayette, CA 94549

Library of Congress Control Number: 2025020403

Printed in China

10 9 8 7 6 5 4 3 2 1

Introduction

ABOUT THIS BOOK

If you are reading this book, you're a quilter—which means that unless you're either brand new to the art or extraordinarily disciplined, you have a bin (or two, or three, or more) of scraps sitting around, and maybe a bunch of fat quarters and smaller cuts of fabrics that you love but don't have a project for. And you'd just love to do something with them.

The idea for this book was born when I decided to make a concerted effort to use some of my scraps and small cuts because they were overflowing my new sewing space. As a modern quilter, though, I found that most scrap quilt patterns were too traditional for my taste. Frequently, they require a consistent background fabric and use the scraps in the foreground. Negative space is often built into the block but probably doesn't include scraps. I love including plenty of negative space in my quilts, so the quilts in this book use the scraps primarily in the negative space. In some cases, the existing scrap quilt formula is flipped on its head by using consistent fabrics in the foreground, whereas others use scraps throughout the entire quilt.

What quilters define as a scrap, and what they keep, differs widely. Some keep every last snippet of fabric, and some throw anything smaller than a fat quarter into the scrap bin. This book includes ten projects that use a variety of scrap sizes and amounts, so no matter where you fall on the spectrum, you will find something to make a dent in your stash!

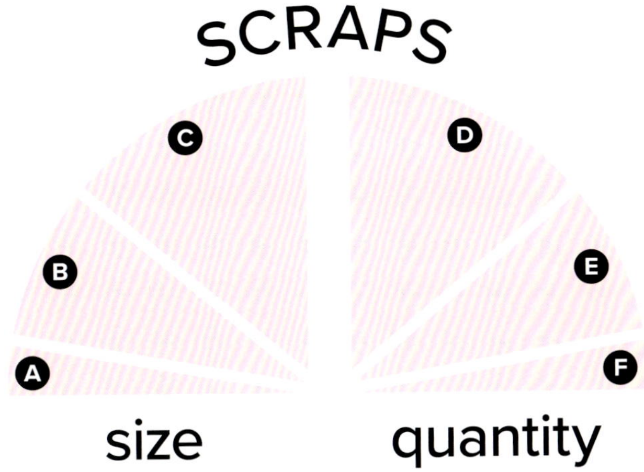

To help you decide which projects your stash is best suited for, each project is rated for the scrap size and the number of scraps you'll need.

A These projects use the smallest scraps: charm squares and smaller. Projects using leftover strips are also included in this category.

B These projects work best with intermediate-size scraps: those between about 5″ and 10″ square.

C These projects use large scraps: such as fat eighths or fat quarters with only a small section used.

D These projects are smaller or use scraps in only a portion of the design. They are good choices for quilters with a limited number of scraps.

E These projects are moderate in size and scrap usage. Quilters with overflowing scrap bins will be able to make a dent in their stash.

F These large projects need a lot of scraps, and you may wish to supplement your scraps with some fat eighths or fat quarters.

Each of the projects uses scraps in a different way, is preceded by a discussion of the way the scraps are used in the negative space, and includes additional ideas for that technique. If you'd rather design your own scrap quilt, you'll find lots of inspiration and suggestions.

Fabric Requirements for Patterns

The fabric requirements for each project are generally given as they would be for standard quilts. If you prefer to use yardage instead of scraps, you'll have the information you need. Depending on the size and shape of the scraps you are working with, you may need to increase the total yardage. The exceptions are the improvisationally pieced quilts in Improvisational Piecing (page 68), where, due to the odd scrap shapes and piecing variation, yardages are by necessity approximate and may not correspond well to nonscrappy blocks.

WHY USE SCRAPS IN NEGATIVE SPACE?

When you use scraps in negative space, the resulting variation in colors and prints gives great depth and added interest to the negative space.

In this version of *Daisy Flower Garden* (page 34), a consistent color is used for the negative space.

Here, using multiple shades of green adds visual interest.

This is just one way of adding interest by using scraps. Using multiple fabrics in the negative space gives you a lot of options for exactly how to add additional interest, which I cover in the following pages. And the benefit to all of this? You'll use a lot of scraps!

EQUIPMENT

Aside from standard quilting supplies, the only thing that is critical for effective scrap quilts is a design wall. You may already have one, but if not, consider adding one to your sewing space. If you don't have the space for a permanent design wall, a number of clever tutorials for portable and retractable design walls are available online. You can also find a friend with a design wall to borrow for a day, or just pin or tape a piece of batting or flannel up for a couple days until you can get your quilt laid out. A "design floor" (in other words, laying your quilt out on the floor) works in a pinch if you have space away from children or pets, who will undoubtedly want to help rearrange your layouts. However, it's harder to step back and get a good view of your quilt when it's on the ground.

A design wall made from insulation boards and covered in flannel

ONLINE RESOURCES

To help you tackle some of the projects in this book, you'll find a refresher on foundation paper piecing and printable templates online. To access this bonus content through the tiny URL, type the web address below into your browser window. To access the content through the QR code, open the camera app on your phone, aim the camera at the QR code, and click the link that pops up on the screen.

tinyurl.com/11606-patterns-download

To use the templates, print directly from the browser window or download the pattern.

- To print at home, print the letter-size pages, selecting 100% size on the printer. Use dashed/dotted lines to trim, layer, and tape together pages as needed.
- To print at a copy shop, save the full-size pages to a thumb drive or email them to your local copy shop for printing.

A NOTE ABOUT TERMINOLOGY

Let's take a moment to define some terminology that is used throughout this book. I refer to the part of the design that draws your eye first as the **foreground**. (Technically, as the opposite of negative space, this is often referred to as "positive space.")

Original design, *Homeward Bound* (page 56)

The **foreground** is highlighted in pink. The **negative space** is the rest of the design—everything else that does not read as the foreground.

I use **background** to refer to an area that recedes completely. Sometimes, this area is one and the same as the negative space, but the negative space may also have layers and include elements on a background.

The **negative space** is highlighted in pink.

The **background** is highlighted in pink.

Free-Form Constellation (page 74) is a design in which the entire negative space reads as background.

The **negative space** and **background**, which are the same in this quilt, are highlighted in pink.

CHAPTER 1

Fabric Choices

BASIC COLOR THEORY

Before we dive into a discussion of different types of fabrics, let's take a moment to review a few definitions that will help you choose fabrics for your scrappy negative space projects.

- A **hue** is a pure color (in painting, a pure pigment, without added white or black).
- **Tints** are created by the addition of white to a hue.
- **Tones** are created by the addition of gray to a hue.
- **Shades** are created by the addition of black to a hue.
- **Value** refers to the lightness or darkness of a color. Tints have a lighter value; shades have a darker value.
- **Color** is the combination of all of these.

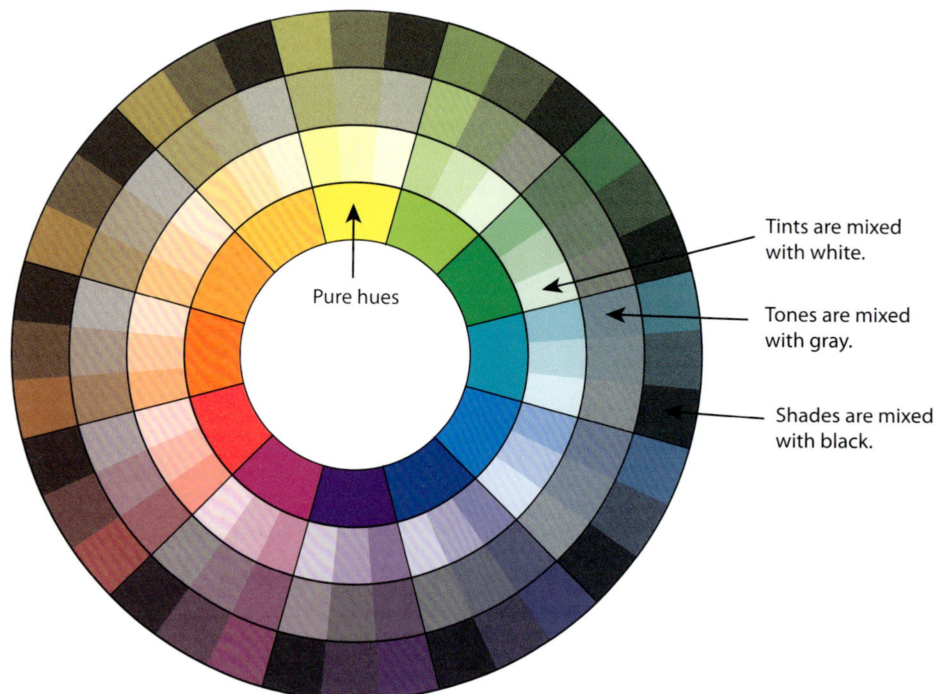

The fabrics quilters tend to call *low-volume* fabrics (low-contrast prints with a white, light gray, or cream background) would more correctly be called *low-value fabrics*. We can probably credit a marketing department somewhere for the alternative term!

That said, value is key in scrap quilts, particularly when using scraps in the negative space. It is, in fact, more important than hue! In the set of four Log Cabin blocks on the left, the two areas to be differentiated are colored in blue and pink, but without regard to the value of the color. Notice how the central blue shape is much harder to see than in the set of blocks on the right, where the central shape has been colored in dark colors and the negative space in light colors. The contrast in value makes the shape visible even without regard to hue (i.e., where it falls on the color wheel, or the rainbow).

Note: Dark shades of yellow and orange end up looking brown, so keep this detail in mind when choosing your color scheme and value placement!

FABRIC CONSIDERATIONS

Oddly enough, scrap quilts are a great place to use your most and your least favorite fabrics. The inclusion of those last beloved little bits of your favorite fabrics will give you a little burst of pleasure whenever you find them hiding in your finished quilt. The small size of many of the pieces, however, means that it is also easy to sneak in fabrics that have been hanging out in your stash for too long because they are not exactly your style anymore. You won't want to use too many of them, lest they become all you see in your finished piece, but scrap quilts are a great place for small quantities of fabrics that you don't care for much or that don't fit into your other quilts. For example, I used to love batiks, but as my quilting style has become more modern, I have moved away from them. Every quilt in this book, though, has at least one batik hiding in it somewhere!

Prints

There are a few considerations to take into account when selecting print fabrics to use in the negative space. First, for the foreground to pop out of the negative space appropriately, there needs to be sufficient contrast between the negative space fabrics and those used in the foreground. This contrast can be achieved by choosing a very different value (i.e., much lighter or darker) for the negative space, by choosing a very different hue, or a combination of the two.

CONTRAST IN PRINT FABRICS

You will also need to consider the contrast between the hues and values within a print fabric. Generally, tone-on-tone fabric will recede into the negative space the best. Multicolor prints can be very difficult to use in negative space if they are not small motifs on a background. They are often intended as the feature fabrics of a collection and, therefore, are by definition attention-grabbing—no wonder they are sometimes called *hero prints*! I recommend saving these types of prints for the foreground or for use in the backing or binding.

These prints have a great deal of variation in hue and value and are designed to draw attention to themselves.

This rainbow of more subtle prints would work better in the negative space.

LOW-VOLUME FABRICS

Be careful with low-volume fabrics in particular to ensure that the prints are not too attention-grabbing. Many fabrics marketed under the low-volume umbrella actually feature black-on-white patterns, which tend to stand out in the negative space. (The same goes for white prints on a dark background, so use them sparingly.) Gray-on-white prints are generally a better and more subtle choice.

In this quilt, *gNOmEL*, some prints in the low-volume scrappy background conflict with the foreground and draw attention away from the trees.

A closeup of the lower-left corner, where numerous high-contrast prints compete with the foreground.

There are times, though, when higher-contrast negative space fabrics can be used judiciously for an interesting effect, such as when you want to emphasize an element in the negative space or if your foreground is extremely different. See Chapter 5: Ghost Blocks (page 52) for an example of black-on-white prints in the negative space.

COLOR ON WHITE PRINTS

Although many low-volume fabrics stick to the tried-and-true gray-and-white formula, some are printed with a single color on white. I find that these are very much worth collecting. They work well for added features of interest in the negative space, such as ghost blocks. You can also add to the mood of your quilt by using them throughout the negative space.

In this quilt, *I Can't Believe I Have to Say This*, the pink-on-white prints used throughout the background add to the feminine mood of the quilt.

Batiks and Hand Dyes

Many batiks are by nature tone-on-tone fabrics and thus work beautifully in negative space. As with prints, be wary of those that include multiple colors, as they can draw too much attention to be effective in the negative space.

Hand-dyed fabrics are perfect for the negative space—their gentle variation in tint is perfect to add texture while not drawing attention to themselves.

At left is a selection of batiks and hand-dyed fabrics that would blend nicely in the negative space. The batiks at right are much bolder and would not work as well.

Solids

If you have scraps of solid fabrics, you can use these too! They are excellent for mixing in with prints to tone down the busyness of the negative space. It is more difficult to use *only* solids in your scrappy negative space, as you need to be careful to keep them from varying too much in hue and value. Try to stick as much as you can to slight variations on the same color—for example, avoid mixing true blues and aqua, unless you are deliberately creating a gradient. See Chapter 10: Foreground Fade-Out (page 104) and Chapter 11: Gradients in the Negative Space (page 114) for more information on gradients.

A good way to select a range of solids that won't vary too much is to use different manufacturers' variations on the same color (for example, "navy" or "royal blue"). This technique will work only for relatively common color names, but it's a starting point! Consider adding a few mottled batiks or hand dyes to round out your selection.

This selection of solids is similar in hue and value and would work well together in the negative space.

ORGANIZING YOUR FABRICS

Sorting Your Stash

When tackling a project from this book or a quilt of your own design that uses scraps in the negative space, you will need to start by sorting through your scraps. If you haven't already done so, sort your scraps by color.

I store my smaller scraps sorted by color in clear plastic bins. (Large scraps stay folded with my fat quarters.)

As we saw earlier, it is best to keep the fabrics in the negative space relatively similar in value. Once you have sorted by color, you can refine your fabric choices by sorting into piles of different values. This categorization doesn't have to be perfect, as some variation in the negative space is fine! If you are worried about whether the fabrics blend well enough, try taking a photo of your scraps; sometimes, it is easier to see whether anything sticks out too much when looking at a photo. You can also try the old trick of making the photo black-and-white, as this method sometimes further highlights fabrics that belong in a different pile or don't fit in with the remaining fabrics in the project.

Fabrics are sorted into piles containing different values of pink. Notice that there is some overlap.

A black-and-white photo reveals some fabrics that are darker in value than the others, particularly in the lightest two piles. If your project requires a particularly consistent background value, these fabrics might have to be omitted; however, a little variation is generally okay in a scrap quilt.

TIP *For quilts that use a gradient, be sure to consult the additional suggestions discussed in Chapter 10: Foreground Fade-Out (page 104) and Chapter 11: Gradients in the Negative Space (page 114)!*

HOW MANY DIFFERENT FABRICS DO I NEED?

If a pattern calls for, say, 50 green 2½″ square scraps, you do *not* need 50 different fabrics! If you have that many, great, but it is also totally okay to cut multiple pieces from one fabric. To preserve a scrappy look, aim to cut no more than about 10 percent of the pieces from any one fabric. In this example, cutting 5 squares from 10 different fabrics is a good option. If you use fewer fabrics, your quilt will look a little more planned and a little less scrappy, which, of course, is okay too!

Purchasing Additional Fabrics

On the other hand, maybe you are not the kind of person who accumulates many scraps. If you want to make some of the projects from this book but don't have enough scraps, try picking up some charm packs or mini charm packs for an easy way to get small amounts of a wider variety of fabrics. Try looking for collections of fabrics in the same color, such as low-volume collections. You could also trade with a friend or organize a swap with your guild.

Packs of 5″ and 2½″ squares

Looking Ahead

No matter where you are in your quilting journey, it's good to periodically reevaluate whether your stash is working for you and whether you need to adjust your purchasing habits.

Begin by taking a look at your recent quilts—all of them, not just the scrappy ones—and ask yourself a couple of questions:

- What kinds of fabrics did you primarily use: solids, blenders, or bold prints?
- How much of each fabric did you use: fat quarters, or did you need a yard or more of each?

If you see yourself continuing in this style of quilting, adjust accordingly—for example, resist picking up fat quarters, tempting as they may be, if you always end up needing more than that. Making some simple rules for yourself can help. My current guidelines for fabric purchases are as follows: If it's a print, do I like it enough to spend the money for a whole yard? If not, it stays at the shop. If it's a solid, I buy a yard at minimum so that I at least have enough for the foreground of a whole quilt.

Most of us go through transitions when our quilting style changes. This shift is totally normal and a sign of your growth as an artist! However, if you find yourself going through a transition, try to put a moratorium on stash building. Buy only what you need for your current project and take notes on what you buy to see whether you can find patterns in your needs. Once you do, you will have a better handle on what you will actually use in future quilts.

Finally, you might find that it is time for a purge of fabrics that no longer work for you. Consider sorting through your stash and either selling or gifting unwanted fabrics to a friend with different fabric tastes or to a guild's charity bee. Some thrift shops love getting donations of craft supplies too!

The Basics

Let's start with the easiest ways of getting some of those scraps used up! The simplest ways of incorporating scraps into the negative space are to just use them for any parts of your block that would be considered background or to use scraps the same size as the blocks for any empty sections.

CHAPTER 2

Scraps in the Block Background

The easiest way to incorporate scraps into your negative space is to use them for the background pieces of quilt blocks. This technique is excellent for quilts with blocks set across the whole quilt, as you may be able to simply use scraps in the negative space without making any changes to the quilt blocks.

This Log Cabin block design could use scraps to create depth in the negative space.

For the quilt to read as "modern," you will want to select a block with plenty of negative space built in and, preferably, with multiple sections of negative space, as in the Log Cabin block above. However, using scraps for block background pieces can be fun even for more traditional designs.

When elements are dropped from the foreground, it often makes sense to just repeat them in the negative space by using scraps. This chapter's project quilt is made up of Pineapple blocks, some of which drop either pink or green pieces. Those fabrics are simply replaced by more low-volume scraps.

In this design inspired by a faded vintage quilt, the "missing" patches are simply replaced by low-volume scraps.

The key to making this technique work is to keep the fabric pieces in the negative space relatively consistent in size. If your quilt design includes large areas of unpieced negative space, you may wish to consider following one of the techniques from subsequent chapters for those areas. Note the differences in the following variation on the Log Cabin design if the negative space is pieced with large sections of fabric versus with relatively consistently sized pieces of fabric (in this case, more Log Cabin blocks). For much more on this technique and ways to make the repetition more prominent, see Chapter 5: Ghost Blocks (page 52).

The negative space does not feel like a logical part of the quilt design when the size of the pieces is not consistent with those nearer the foreground area.

Keeping the size of the fabric pieces in the negative space consistent across the whole quilt helps unify the design.

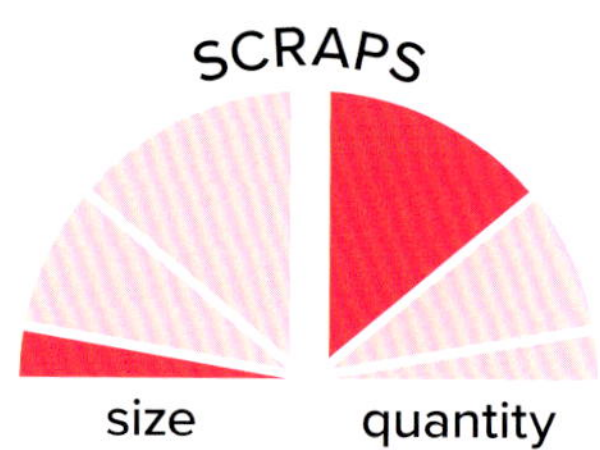

Paradise This Way

Finished block size: 9″ • Finished quilt size: 54½″ × 54½″

This quilt based on the Pineapple block uses consistent foreground fabrics and scraps in the negative space. If you prefer to make your foreground scrappy as well, be sure to check out the fabric-sorting tips in the chapters on color gradients, starting on page 102.

Materials

Yardages are based on 40″-wide fabric.

Yellow: ⅜ yard for block centers

Light pink (Pink 1): ⅜ yard

Medium-light pink (Pink 2): ⅜ yard

Medium-dark pink (Pink 3): ⅜ yard

Dark pink (Pink 4): ¾ yard for block corners

Light green (Green 1): ¼ yard

Medium-light green (Green 2): ¼ yard

Medium-dark green (Green 3): ¼ yard

Dark green (Green 4): ⅝ yard for block corners

Low-volume scraps: equivalent of 3½ yards for block background

Binding: ½ yard

Backing: 3½ yards

Batting: 62½″ × 62½″

ADDITIONAL MATERIALS

Make 36 copies of the Paradise This Way paper-piecing template (pages 28–29) on foundation paper and tape them together on the indicated line. If you don't feel like photocopying the template, you can download and print it by going to Online Resources (page 9).

Designed, pieced, and quilted by Sylvia Schaefer

CUTTING

Yellow

Cut 3 strips 2½″ × width of fabric (WOF); subcut into 36 squares 2½″ × 2½″ for block centers (Piece 1).

Light Pink (Pink 1)

Cut 6 strips 1½″ × WOF; subcut into 56 strips 1½″ × 3½″ for blocks (Pieces 8 and 9).

Medium-Light Pink (Pink 2)

Cut 6 strips 1½″ × WOF; subcut into 56 strips 1½″ × 4″ for blocks (Pieces 16 and 17).

Medium-Dark Pink (Pink 3)

Cut 7 strips 1½″ × WOF; subcut into 56 strips 1½″ × 5″ for blocks (Pieces 24 and 25).

Dark Pink (Pink 4)

Cut 4 strips 5″ × WOF; subcut into 28 squares 5″ × 5″ for block corners; cut the squares in half diagonally. (Pieces 32 and 33).

Light Green (Green 1)

Cut 4 strips 1½″ × WOF; subcut into 40 strips 1½″ × 3½″ for blocks (Pieces 6 and 7).

Medium-Light Green (Green 2)

Cut 4 strips 1½″ × WOF; subcut into 40 strips 1½″ × 4″ for blocks (Pieces 14 and 15).

Medium-Dark Green (Green 3)

Cut 5 strips 1½″ × WOF; subcut into 40 strips 1½″ × 5″ for blocks (Pieces 22 and 23).

CUTTING continued on next page

Dark Green (Green 4)

Cut 3 strips 5″ × WOF; subcut into 20 squares 5″ × 5″ for block corners; cut the squares in half diagonally (Pieces 30 and 31).

Low-volume scraps

For the background:

Cut 72 squares 2½″ × 2½″; cut the squares in half diagonally (Pieces 2–5).

Cut 192 strips 1½″ × 3½″ (Pieces 6–13).

Cut 192 strips 1½″ × 4″ (Pieces 14–21).

Cut 192 strips 1½″ × 5″ (Pieces 22–29).

Cut 24 squares 5″ × 5″; cut the squares in half diagonally (Pieces 30–33).

CONSTRUCTION

Block Assembly

1. Paper piece the blocks, following the color indications on the template for Block A (12 blocks). For Block B (16 blocks), substitute background scraps for the green fabrics. For Block C (8 blocks), substitute background scraps for the pink fabrics.

Note: If you need a refresher on paper piecing, jump to Online Resources (page 9) to download a tutorial.

Block A: Make 12.

Block B: Make 16.

Block C: Make 8.

TIP **STAYING ORGANIZED** • *Use a pen to note directly on the foundation paper where you are using background instead of pink or green. (And be careful not to accidentally grab your heat-erase pen to do so! Ask me how I know…)*

2. Trim the blocks to the outside line and remove the papers.

Quilt Assembly

Following the assembly diagram, sew the blocks together in rows, paying careful attention to the orientation of the blocks. Sew the rows together.

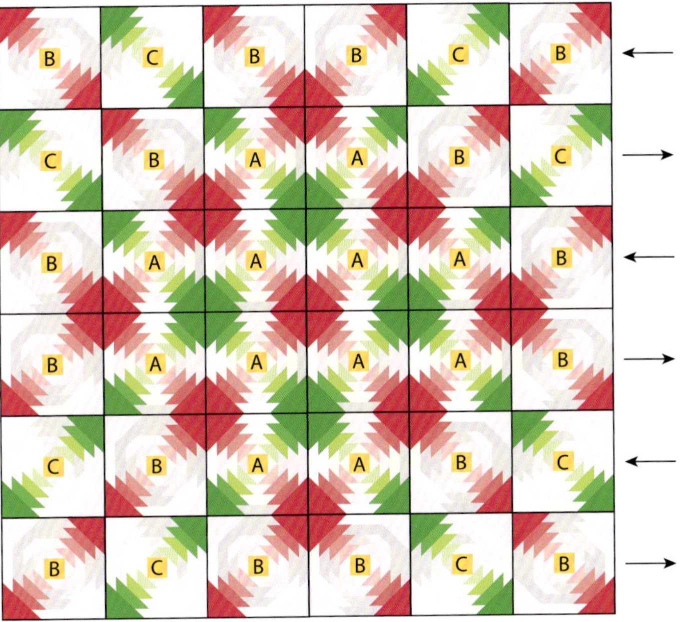

Quilt assembly diagram: Arrows indicate pressing direction.

FINISHING

1. Divide the backing into 2 lengths 62½″ long. Trim selvedges and sew the pieces together along the long side. Trim to 62½″ × 62½″.

2. Layer, baste, and quilt as desired.

3. Cut 6 strips 2″ × WOF (or up to 2½″ wide, as desired) from the binding fabric and piece together with diagonal seams. Press in half lengthwise and finish the quilt with a double-fold binding.

The sample was quilted with the *Pineapple Flowers* pantograph by Hermione Agee of Lorien Quilting.

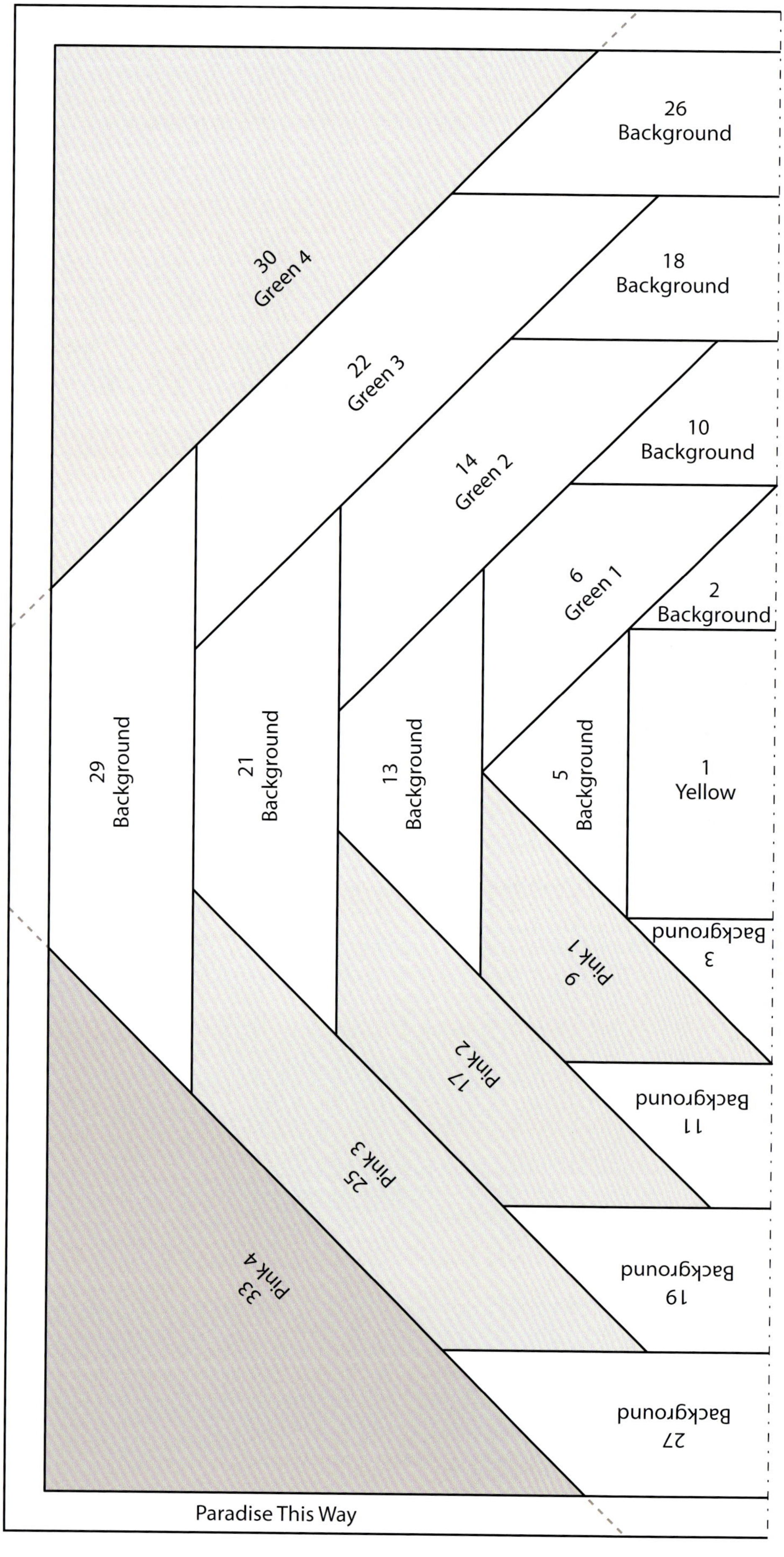

26
Background

30
Green 4

18
Background

22
Green 3

10
Background

14
Green 2

6
Green 1

2
Background

29
Background

21
Background

13
Background

5
Background

1
Yellow

3
Background

9
Pink 1

17
Pink 2

11
Background

25
Pink 3

19
Background

33
Pink 4

27
Background

Paradise This Way

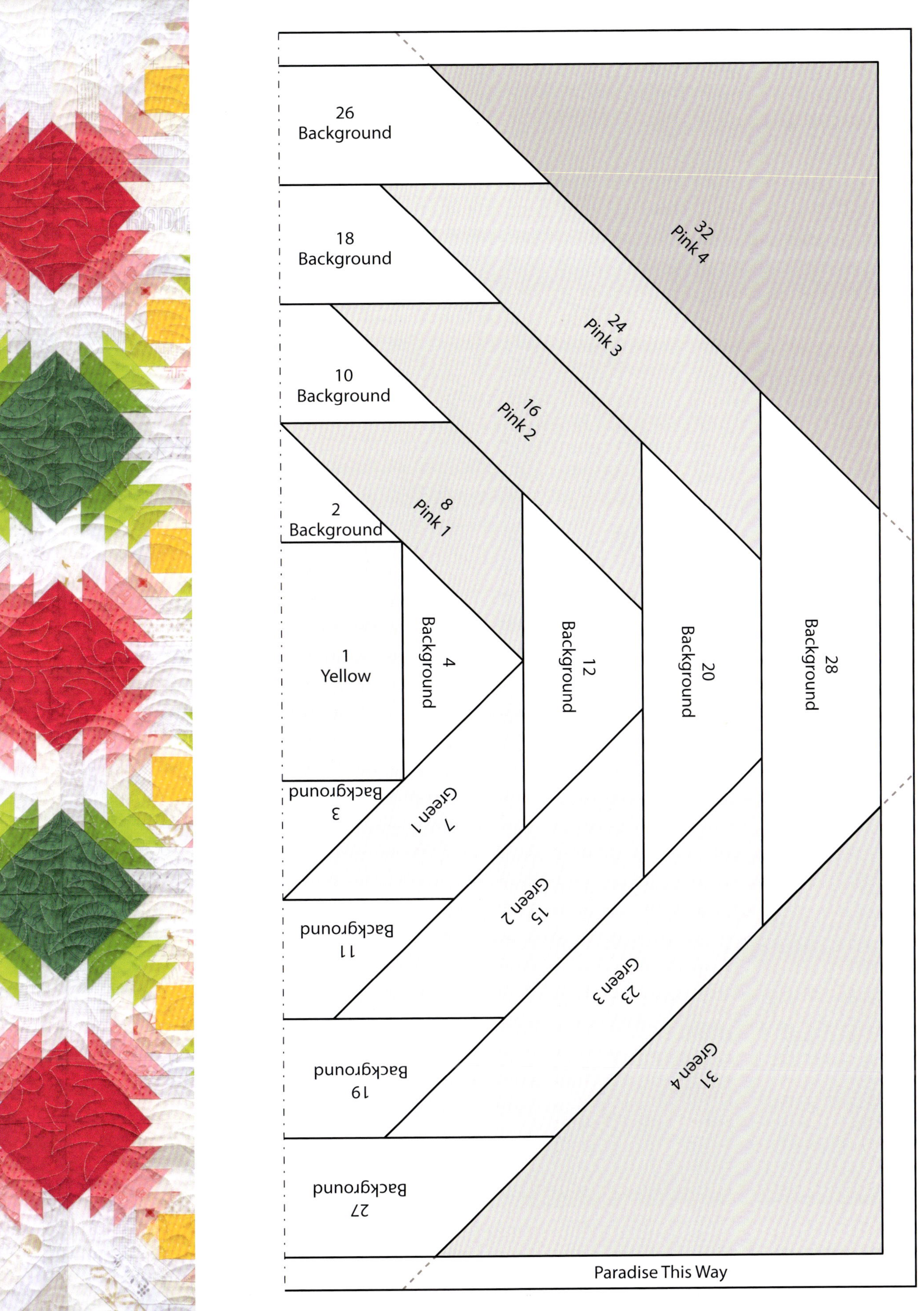

26
Background
18
Background
10
Background
2
Background
1
Yellow
3
Background
11
Background
19
Background
27
Background
4
Background
8
Pink 1
16
Pink 2
24
Pink 3
32
Pink 4
12
Background
20
Background
28
Background
7
Green 1
15
Green 2
23
Green 3
31
Green 4
Paradise This Way

CHAPTER 3
Echoing Block Shapes

If your quilt design includes negative space outside the blocks, a simple way of making it scrappy is to repeat the block shape throughout the negative space. Because this technique will make your foreground appear to be floating atop a mosaic pattern, be sure to keep the negative-space fabric consistent within each foreground block as well.

SQUARE BLOCKS

If your blocks are square, use your scraps to cut squares the same size as the blocks for use in the negative space.

This method is generally most effective where the blocks are small and the negative space is not a key element of the block, in part because the technique is best if the quilt includes a lot of blocks. It is also very effective when the quilt design contains negative space throughout.

This design includes multiple areas of negative space.

In contrast, recall the Log Cabin block example from the previous chapter. Here, just using large squares still leaves an unsatisfactory appearance because the negative space is so integral to the Log Cabin block.

See Chapter 2: Scraps in the Block Background (page 22) for a more effective version of this design!

If the block size is on the larger side, try setting the blocks on point instead. This placement can significantly improve the appearance of plain squares in the negative space.

A Dresden Plate design with repeated squares as the negative space

The same quilt design, but blocks are rotated to be on point

Although modern quilts rarely use sashing, this technique can work with quilts that do so. In this case, you would choose whether to use scraps in the blocks, sashing, or both.

Variation in the blocks only

Variation in the sashing only

Variation in the blocks and the sashing. Note that the color value is different for the sashing and blocks (i.e., the block backgrounds are darker than the sashings), so they are still easily distinguishable.

OTHER SHAPES

Echoed negative-space blocks really shine with nonsquare block shapes. This chapter's project, *Daisy Flower Garden* (page 34) features hexagonal blocks repeated across the whole quilt; other sorts of quadrilaterals (four-sided shapes) and triangles also work.

This example is just one of many interesting triangle-shaped blocks to explore.

Alternate Grids

If the geometry permits, varying the block size creates additional interest in the negative space. This technique may also provide a greater variety of options for the placement of your foreground blocks, allowing you to fine-tune exactly where you want them while also adding interest by varying the size. However, this style works only for a limited number of block shapes: primarily triangles, squares, and rectangles.

An alternate-grid quilt design using multiple block sizes

Multishape Tessellations

If you want to get really creative, repeating block shapes in the negative space can include tessellations of multiple shapes. Sometimes, this placement does not even require creative piecing, as with octagons and squares, where you can piece your blocks as squares that form a secondary design when assembled.

A grid of square blocks that appear octagonal due to color placement

If your tessellations are particularly complex, you may not want to do any additional piecing within the blocks, particularly if the blocks are small. Color or fabric choices alone can create the foreground with plain block shapes. This type of pattern is great for English paper piecing!

A galaxy-inspired quilt design using a Penrose tessellation, with plain blocks in the foreground and the negative space

Finally, if you are looking for an interesting background for large-scale appliqué, just piecing large block shapes is one of several techniques in this book that would be effective!

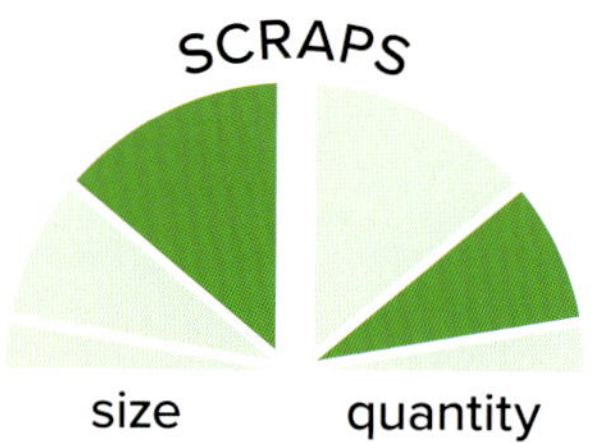

Daisy Flower Garden

Finished block size: 13⅞″ × 12″ • Finished quilt size: 56″ × 72½″

This project is great for using up fat quarters with just a little "bite" cut out of them. If you have a range of values to use in the negative space, consider a gradient from light to dark as in the sample quilt—see Chapter 11: Gradients in the Negative Space (page 114) for more on this idea!

Choose a lighter and a darker fabric for each of the flowers. By placing slightly lighter petals in front and slightly darker petals in back, you create depth in the flower.

The base of this quilt is sewn together first, and then the flowers are appliquéd on top. Instructions for hand or invisible machine appliqué are included here, but you can use another appliqué method if you prefer.

Materials

Yardages are based on 40″-wide fabric.

Assorted greens: 30 scraps 15″ × 13″, or equivalent of 4¼ yards, for background

Petal fabrics: ⅛ yard each of 32 fabrics, consisting of 16 pairs of light and dark same-color fabrics

White solid: ⅛ yard for flower centers

Binding: ⅝ yard

Backing: 3⅝ yards. *NOTE: Assumes 42″-wide fabric*

Batting: 64″ × 80½″

Scraps of template plastic for appliqué placement

Freezer paper, liquid starch, and washable fabric glue, or the appliqué supplies needed for your preferred method

Note: For the medium and small flowers, you will need only about half of the indicated flower fabric size. A large scrap, such as a 10″ square, can be used.

Designed, pieced, and quilted by Sylvia Schaefer

CUTTING

Green Scraps

From each scrap, cut 2 strips 6½″ by at least 15″ long. Trim the first short end to 60° by using the 60° line on your ruler (shown in red). Cut along the edge shown in blue.

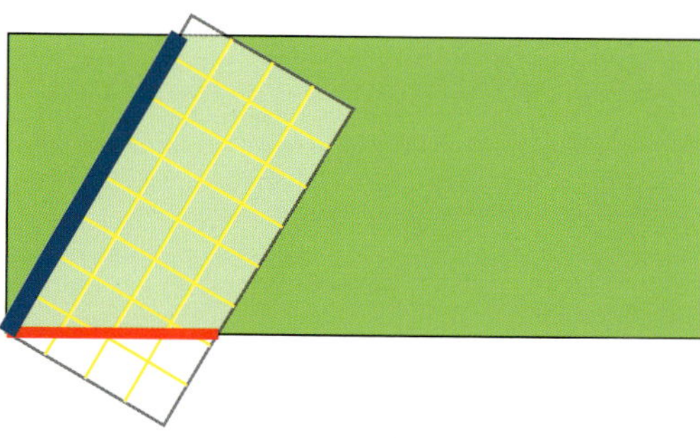

Measure 7¼″ along the top edge and make a small mark with a fabric-marking pen.

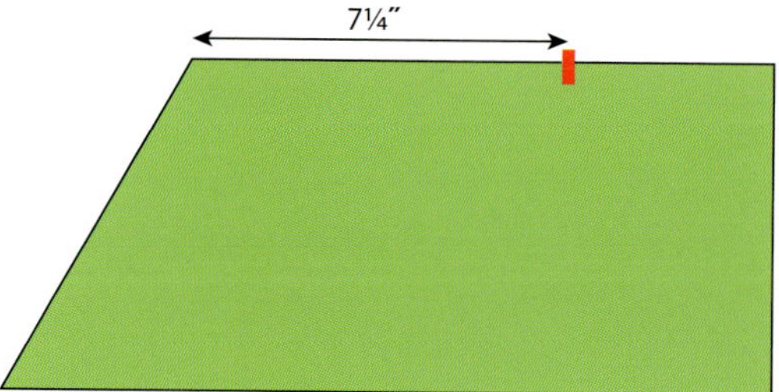

CUTTING continued on next page

Align the 60° line on your ruler (shown in red) with the top edge of your fabric, placing the cutting edge (shown in blue) right at the 7¼″ mark. Make the second cut.

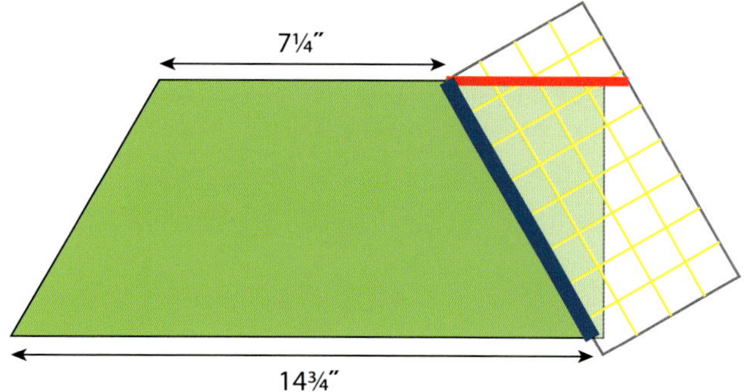

Repeat to make a second half hexagon from the second strip.

TIP *If any of your background greens are directional fabric and you're the type of quilter who cares about the orientation, be sure to cut 1 half hexagon right side up and the second one upside down.*

Cut 28 pairs of half hexagons (for the full blocks) and 4 single half hexagons (for the half blocks at the top and bottom of the quilt), for a total of 60 half hexagons.

Note: If you'd prefer a template to the measuring method presented here, go to Online Resources (page 9) to download a template for the background half hexagons.

Petal Fabrics and White Solid

For the appliqué, you can photocopy or trace the Daisy Flower Garden templates included here, or you can download and print the templates. To access the downloadable versions, go to Online Resources (page 9).

Appliqué Methods

You may use whatever method you prefer to prepare and apply the appliqué pieces. I stitched mine by hand, but you could also sew the turned-edge pieces by machine or use fusible web to make raw-edge appliqué. The templates do not include a seam allowance, so if your preferred method requires a seam allowance, be sure to add it when cutting your appliqué pieces. You do not need to add seam allowance to the flat bottoms of the flower petals, as these will be underneath the center hexagons.

PETAL FABRICS

Using the provided templates, cut 6 large petals from each of 7 pairs of petal fabric, cut 6 medium petals from each of 6 pairs of petal fabric, and cut 6 small petals from each of 3 pairs of petal fabric, for a total of 12 petals per block.

WHITE FLOWER CENTERS

Using the provided templates, cut 7 large flower centers, 6 medium flower centers, and 3 small flower centers.

CONSTRUCTION

Hexagon Assembly

1. Using a design wall and referring to the hexagon assembly diagram, lay out your half hexagons.

Hexagon assembly: Arrows indicate pressing direction.

Alternative Assembly

If you are comfortable with Y-seams and would prefer to appliqué onto smaller pieces of fabric, you could assemble the hexagons, appliqué the flowers, and then sew the hexagons together with Y-seams.

2. Sew the half hexagons together in rows. Align the half hexagons so that a small triangle is overhanging approximately ¼″ on either end.

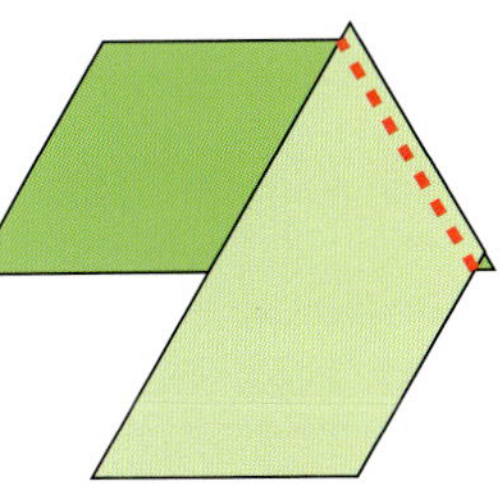

3. Sew the rows together.

TIP *Zigzag stitch around the edge of the quilt to secure the seams and reduce fraying, as you will be handling the quilt top a fair bit to appliqué the flowers.*

Appliqué

If you're turning the appliqué edges ahead of time (such as with freezer paper and liquid starch), do so now.

PLACING THE APPLIQUÉ PIECES

1. Trace the center hexagon templates onto a piece of template plastic, including the inner dashed placement line and the center dot.

2. For each block that will contain a flower, mark reference lines across the block from each corner to the opposite corner and from the center of each edge to the center of the opposite edge. (Your seam serves as one of these lines, so you don't need to mark that one.)

Note: For blocks on the edge of the quilt, the marking lines need to start at the seam allowance line rather than at the edge of the quilt. Measure in ¼″ from the edge to find the correct starting point.

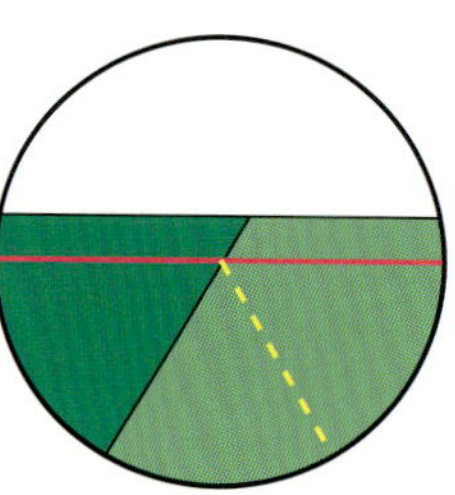

3. Place the appropriate (large, medium, or small) plastic hexagon template in the center of the block, with the corners on the lines connecting the centers of the block.

4. Slide the bottom (darker) petals underneath, lining up the bottom edge with the dotted line on the hexagon template and lining up the top points with the marked lines on the quilt. Secure them to the quilt with pins or a few dots of washable glue.

5. Hand stitch or, using an open-toed appliqué foot, stitch down the bottom petals with a narrow zigzag stitch, just catching the edge of the appliqué piece. Pull out the freezer paper toward the end of each stitching.

6. Place the hexagon template back in the center of the block, but rotate it so that now the corners are lined up on the lines connecting the corners of the block.

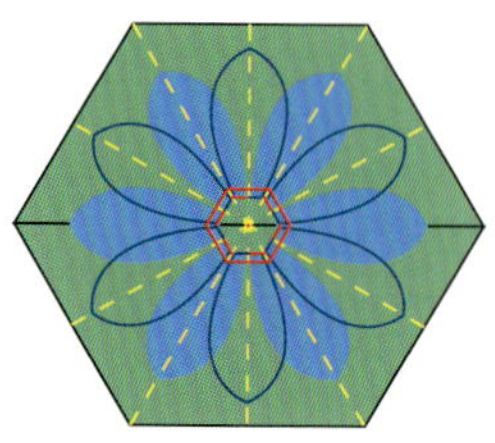

7. Slide the top (lighter) petals underneath, lining up the bottom edge with the dashed line on the hexagon template and lining up the top points with the marked lines on the quilt. Secure them to the quilt with pins or a few dots of washable glue.

8. Hand stitch or, using an open-toed appliqué foot, stitch down the top petals with a narrow zigzag stitch, just catching the edge of the appliqué piece. Pull out the freezer paper toward the end of each stitching.

9. Place the center hexagon on the block and stitch it down.

10. Repeat Steps 2–9 to appliqué the remaining blocks.

Small (S), Medium (M), and Large (L) flowers are arranged across the quilt top.

FINISHING

1. Divide the backing into 2 lengths 64″ long. Trim selvedges and sew the pieces together along the long side. Trim to 64″ × 80½″.

2. Layer, baste, and quilt as desired.

TIP *The scraps in this quilt are on the larger side, so they are better able to support custom quilting. With less variation in prints, the quilting stitches are less likely to get lost. Echo quilting some of the motifs also helps the visibility.*

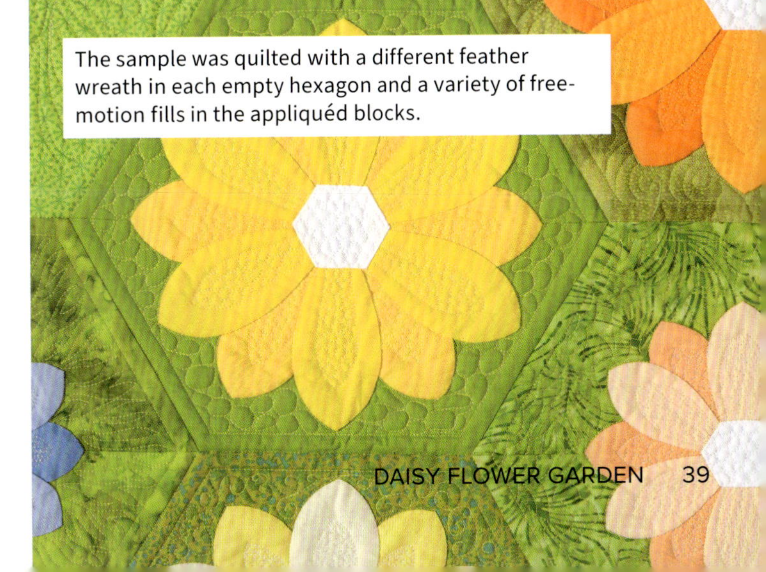

The sample was quilted with a different feather wreath in each empty hexagon and a variety of free-motion fills in the appliquéd blocks.

Binding

1. Cut 7 strips 2″ × width of fabric (WOF) (or up to 2½″, as desired) from the binding fabric and piece them together with diagonal seams. Press in half lengthwise.

2. Beginning along the top edge of the quilt, start applying the binding.

3. Outside corners are handled just like typical quilt corners, just at a different angle. When you reach the first corner, stop stitching ¼″ from the edge.

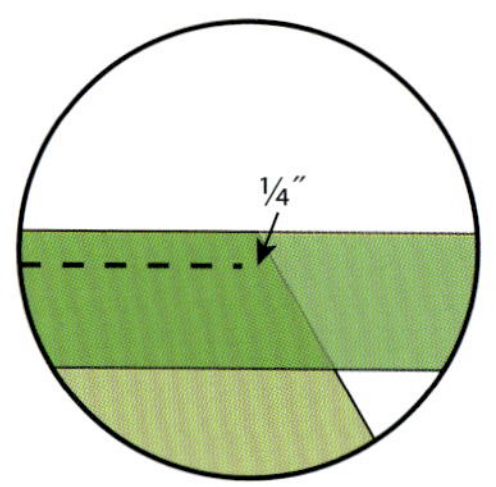

4. Fold the binding back so the open edge is parallel with the second edge.

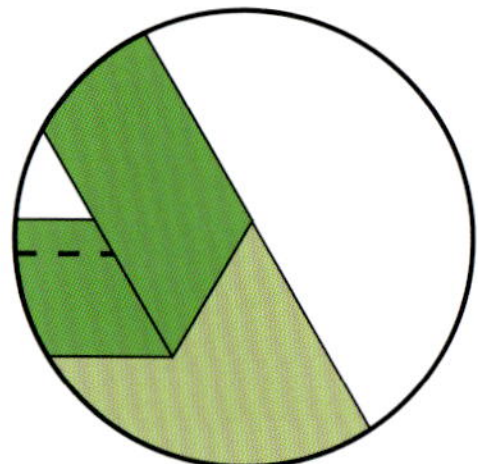

5. Keeping the first fold in place, fold the binding again so it is now on top of the second edge.

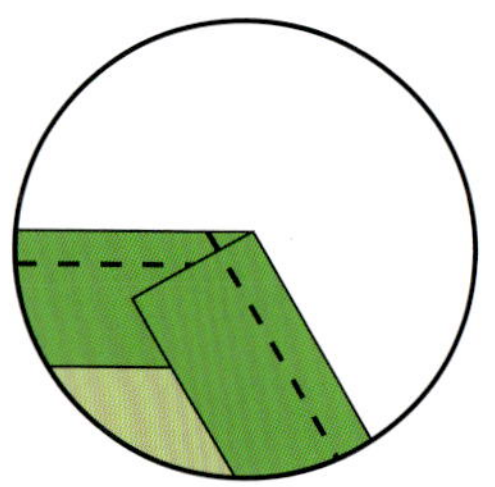

6. Continue applying the binding starting at the top edge. It is a good idea to make a few backstitches here.

7. When you arrive at an inside corner, stop stitching right on the seam between hexagons, leaving the needle in the down position.

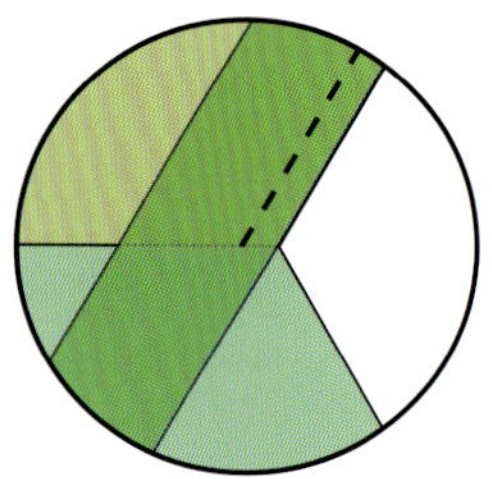

8. Shift the quilt so that you are ready to continue stitching along the edge and pull the binding around the needle so that it is parallel to the next edge; then, continue stitching. The binding will bunch around the needle, so a stiletto is very useful here to ensure that you are not accidentally stitching any tucks or folds into the binding.

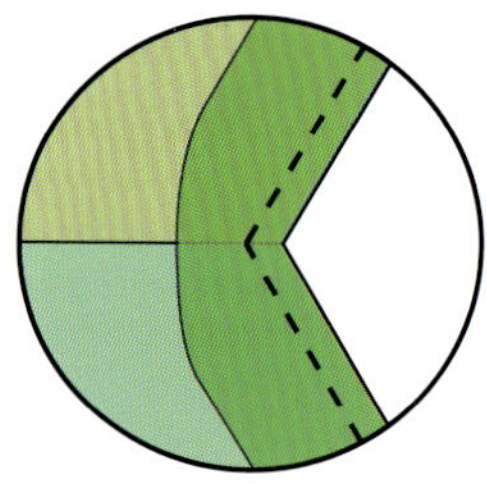

9. Continue stitching around the quilt, mitering at each outside corner and pulling at the inside corners. When you reach the top edge again, join the binding ends by using your favorite technique.

10. Fold the binding to the back of the quilt and hand stitch it down.

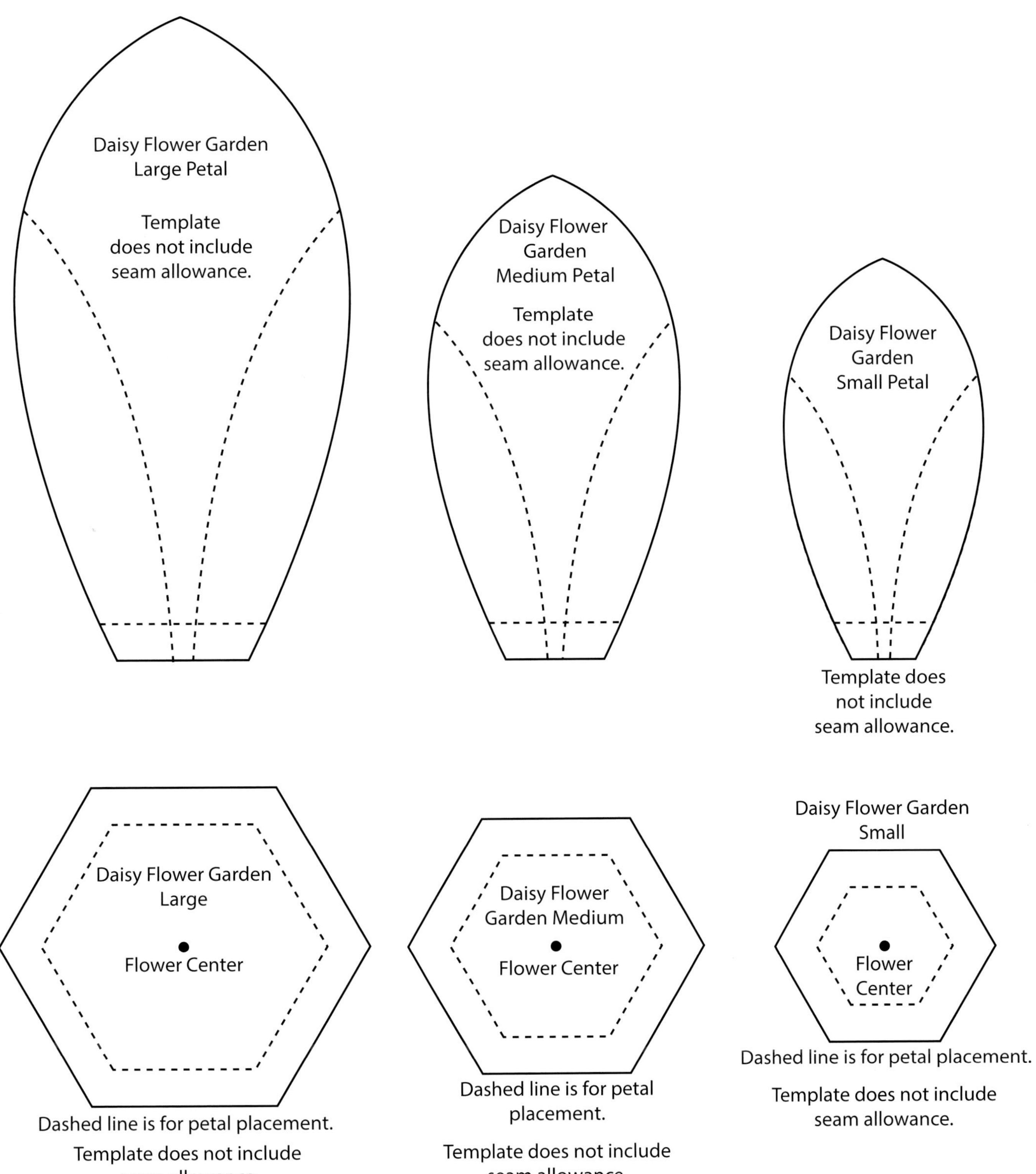
Daisy Flower Garden
Large Petal
Template
does not include
seam allowance.
Daisy Flower
Garden
Medium Petal
Template
does not include
seam allowance.
Daisy Flower
Garden
Small Petal
Template does
not include
seam allowance.
Daisy Flower Garden
Large
Flower Center
Daisy Flower
Garden Medium
Flower Center
Daisy Flower Garden
Small
Flower
Center
Dashed line is for petal placement.
Template does not include
seam allowance
Dashed line is for petal
placement.
Template does not include
seam allowance.
Dashed line is for petal placement.
Template does not include
seam allowance.

Filling in Blocks

The next three chapters show you how to fill in the negative space with traditional blocks. Whether it is piecing the same block as the foreground or a contrasting choice, using traditional blocks in the negative space ups the interest factor but keeps the assembly straightforward. There is considerable overlap between these chapters, so be sure to read through all of them before finalizing your designs using traditional blocks in the negative space!

CHAPTER 4

Accent Blocks

Incorporating scrappy accents into the negative space of a quilt design is a good choice when you have only a limited number of scraps. Rather than using scraps for the entirety of the negative space, as so many of the other designs in this book do, in this chapter, these designs use a consistent background fabric for most of the negative space. The accents add little pops of interest.

TYPES OF ACCENTS

These accents can be whole blocks, parts of blocks, or just small pieces of fabrics, and they can either blend with the background or contrast with it.

Whole Blocks

Adding a few whole blocks into the negative space can help connect the negative space to the foreground. Whole blocks in the background can be awkward, however, as they can appear isolated without a clear connection to the remainder of the blocks.

Although the inclusion of yellow blocks in the foreground helps, it is unclear why the two squircle blocks are floating on top of the background in this example.

Taking a few blocks away from the foreground and extending part of it upward and downward introduces an element of disintegration or deconstruction, and the blocks feel more intentional. Here, only the yellow squircles are scrappy, but the purple ones—or just a few select purple ones—could be made scrappy as well.

Block Parts

If whole-block accents in the negative space don't give the desired look, try using just whichever part of the block catches your attention!

Two versions of the same quilt design—in the first, block parts blend with the background; in the second, they contrast.

Small Fabric Pieces

Small pieces, especially small irregular fabric pieces, can also work as accents in the negative space. This style of accent provides more of a confetti-type look and could be a fun choice for birthday or celebration quilts. This style of accent will most likely involve improvisational piecing of the background.

Triangle accents in the negative space echo the triangle shapes in the foreground Mariner's Compass block. More have been placed toward the bottom to emphasize the effect of falling confetti.

Hybrids

There are some intermediates between whole blocks and block parts as well. One such intermediate is the use of smaller blocks as accents in the negative space.

Using successively smaller stars toward the outside of the quilt draws attention inward.

Using whole blocks *and* block parts is another option. Here, it is generally best to use only a few whole blocks and stick with block parts for the majority of the negative space.

In this alternative version of this chapter's project, *Chocolate and Sprinkles* (page 48), accent H blocks using different fabrics are incorporated into the background.

ACCENT PLACEMENT

Accents do not have to just be scattered across the quilt top; they can be placed in an organized pattern, such as in lines. This arrangement can create visual depth in the quilt design by appearing to form layers if these organized patterns of accents intersect with foreground piecing.

The simple diamond shapes in this block are extended into the negative space as contrasting lines of accents. Varying the length of the lines provides a little bit of asymmetry.

ACCENT FABRIC CHOICES

In some of the examples above, the accents blend with the background to form part of the negative space. In these cases, be sure to choose a solid or a very subtle print as the background fabric so the accents still draw a little bit more attention than the background.

Where the accents contrast, they tend to be seen as part of the foreground, so there is some more flexibility in what works well as a background print. As for the accents themselves, you can opt for bolder fabric choices because the accents are designed to draw attention. Keep such bold accents small, though, so that there is still plenty of negative space to allow the eye to rest.

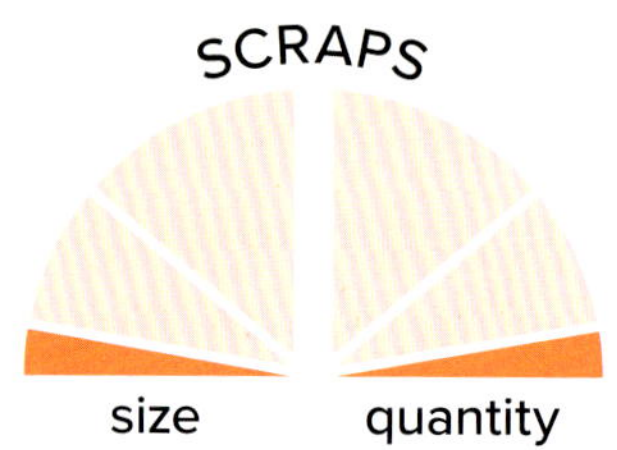

Chocolate and Sprinkles

Finished block size: 6″ • Finished quilt size: 60½″ × 84½″

This project is great if you have only a limited number of scraps or if you have already precut your scraps into 2½″ squares. Feel free to use a range of values from light to dark in the scraps; the design does not depend on keeping them consistent. The quilt reminds me of the Pop-Tarts I lived on in college and of being mugged for them by astonishingly brazen squirrels on the steps of the music building. See if you can spot the little marauders in my quilt!

Materials

Yardages are based on 40″-wide fabric.

Brown solid: 1⅝ yards

Light pink solid: 3 yards for background

Pink scraps: equivalent of ⅜ yard for blocks and accents

Orange scraps: equivalent of ⅜ yard for blocks and accents

Yellow scraps: equivalent of ⅜ yard for blocks and accents

Green scraps: equivalent of ⅜ yard for blocks and accents

Binding: ⅝ yard

Backing: 5¼ yards

Batting: 68½″ × 92½″

Designed, pieced, and quilted by Sylvia Schaefer

CUTTING

Brown Solid

Cut 21 strips 2½″ × width of fabric (WOF); subcut into:

- 106 strips 2½″ × 6½″
- 53 squares 2½″ × 2½″

Light Pink Solid

Cut 40 strips 2½″ × WOF; subcut into:

- 174 strips 2½″ × 6½″
- 71 strips 2½″ × 4½″
- 25 squares 2½″ × 2½″

Pink Scraps

Cut 51 squares 2½″ × 2½″.

Orange Scraps

Cut 49 squares 2½″ × 2½″.

Yellow Scraps

Cut 52 squares 2½″ × 2½″.

Green Scraps

Cut 50 squares 2½″ × 2½″.

CONSTRUCTION

Block Assembly

1. Sew the scraps into 6½″ strips, as indicated in the diagram. For strip sets with 3 colors, use 3 squares 2½″ × 2½″. For strip sets with a pale pink background and only 1 color of scrap, sew a 2½″ × 4½″ strip to the square of the corresponding color.

2. Add a 2½″ × 6½″ strip that matches the center to the top and bottom of each strip set to make the number of blocks indicated in the diagram.

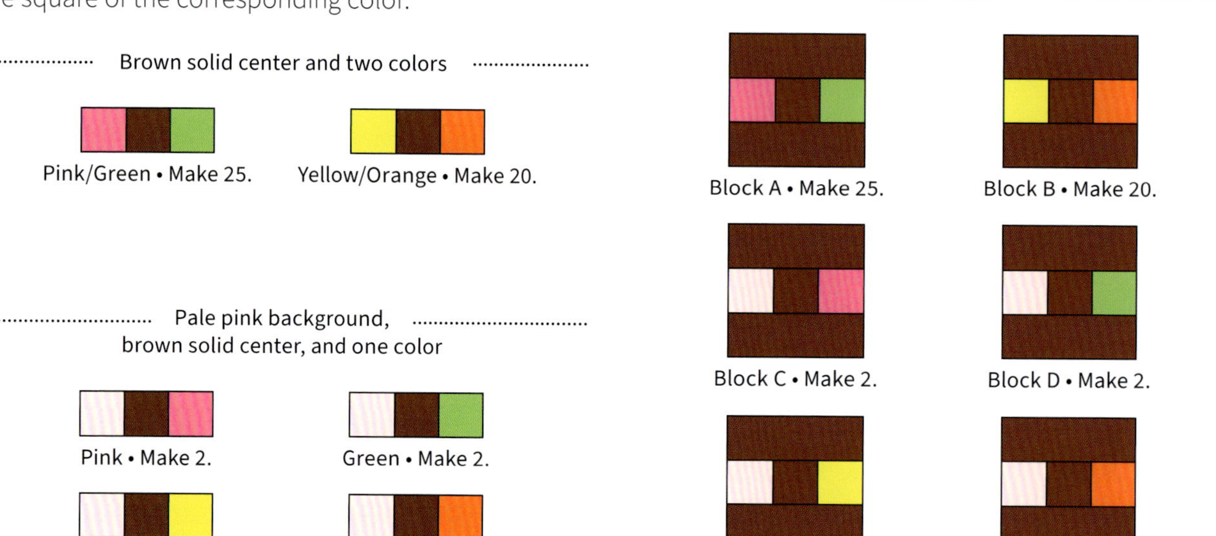

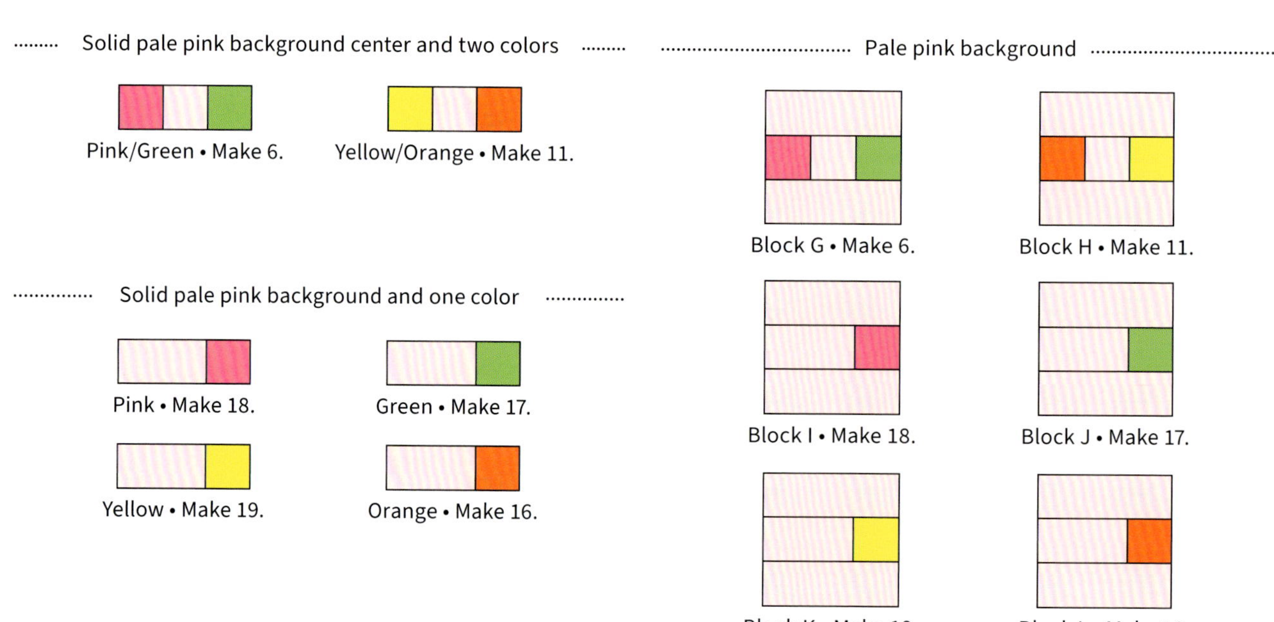

Quilt Assembly

1. Following the assembly diagram, sew the blocks together in rows, paying careful attention to the orientation of the blocks. Sew the rows together.

Quilt assembly diagram: Arrows indicate pressing direction.

FINISHING

1. Divide the backing into 2 lengths 92½″ long. Trim selvedges and sew the pieces together along the long side. (This seam will run vertically down the backing.) Trim to 68½″ × 92½″.

2. Layer, baste, and quilt as desired.

3. Cut 8 strips 2″ × WOF (or up to 2½″, as desired) from the binding fabric and piece together with diagonal seams. Press in half lengthwise and finish the quilt with a double-fold binding.

The sample was quilted with the *Dave's Buttercup* pantograph, with a few *Dave's Squirrels* motifs sprinkled in (both by Dave Hudson).

CHAPTER 5

Ghost Blocks

BLOCK PLACEMENT

An excellent way to keep the negative space integrated with your design is to simply echo the block shapes in the negative space. You can do this by using what I like to call *ghost blocks*—toned-down versions of the foreground blocks. These blocks can be the same size and placement as the foreground blocks, or you can change the sizes to be smaller or larger (or a mix of the two!) for an interesting contrast.

These blocks do not have to fill the entire negative space—in fact, leaving some space clear of piecing altogether can help open the quilt design further. If you combine this style with the variation in value afforded by using scraps, you can create an interesting fade-out effect that provides an almost three-dimensional appearance.

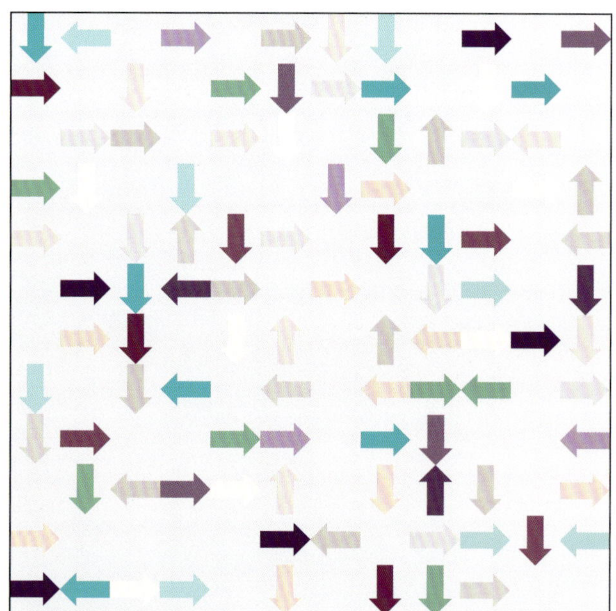

The empty spaces in this design blend into the lightest ghost blocks to produce visual depth.

FABRIC SELECTION

You have a variety of options when considering what fabrics to use for these ghost blocks. The simplest possibility is to use similar scraps without particular regard to fabric placement, like what was discussed in Chapter 2: Scraps in the Block Background (page 22). This method will result in a subtle repetition of the block in the negative space area.

The whole negative space is filled with circle blocks.

To make the ghost blocks a little more prominent, use colors similar (slightly lighter or darker) to your background fabric. For example, on a white background, use light grays; on a black background, you could use very dark grays. You can also use paler versions of your main block colors. If you're using a white or light background, opt for very light versions (tints) of your main colors. If you're using black or a dark background, look for very deep shades.

Light background, ghosts similar to background

Dark background, ghosts similar to background

Mid-tone background, ghosts similar to background

Light background, ghosts colored

Dark background, ghosts colored

Mid-tone background, ghosts colored

If you're using something in between, particularly another color, this technique will be a little more difficult, as you will need to find tones (those are the colors that mix hues with gray). The concept of *transparency* is very useful here. Imagine that in the negative space, your ghost blocks are actually transparent and resting on the background. You will need to find colors that are in between the foreground and the background to create this effect. The closer to opposite your two colors are, the grayer and muddier the mixed color will be. So although it seems counterintuitive, you may still need those gray and neutral fabrics, even when your foreground and your background are colorful!

The colors in the outer and center rings are overlaid in the middle section of this illustration. These colors are opposite one another on the color wheel; overlaying them results in grayish, muddy tones.

Print Considerations

Solids or tone-on-tone prints are always great choices for your scrappy ghost blocks, but this case is one where you may be able to get away with using bolder prints, if you choose them carefully.

For example, black-on-white prints are often too bold to blend well into low-volume negative space—when you're squinting or taking a black-and-white photograph of your selections, they often stick out as being too dark in value. However, if you choose a white background and piece ghost blocks out of these types of fabric, the white will flow into the background, leaving only black partial shapes. This choice actually creates an interesting optical illusion for which your brain completes the shapes!

The black-on-white print on a white background doesn't actually put triangles in the negative space—but you still see them!

If you have a colorful bold print you'd like to consider for the ghost blocks, pair it with a solid the same color as a prominent element or the background of your ghost block fabric to create the same partial triangle effect that will allow the ghosts to read as negative space rather than as a secondary main element. You may also want to keep the piecing at a smaller scale so elements from the print are cut up and, therefore, less recognizable.

Choosing a matching background fabric for this bold print tones it down to the point where you might be able to use it as a ghost block.

On a white background, another option is low-volume fabrics with a colorful print. These fabrics can read as very light tints of the print color and so can be interesting choices for the ghost-block technique in particular (see also Chapter 1: Fabric Choices, page 12).

A star block from low-volume fabric with a red print

When in doubt, try sewing a test block with your chosen fabrics to check how they work!

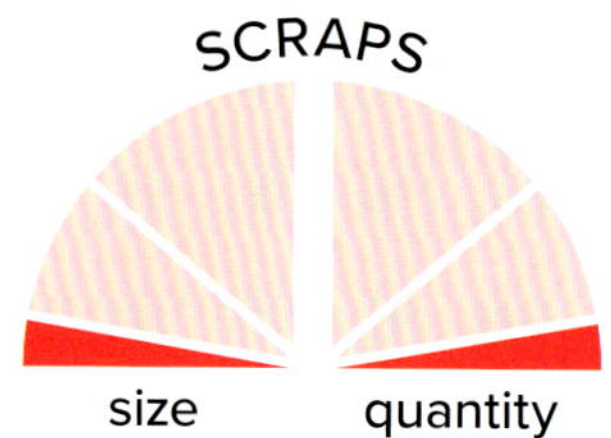

Materials

Yardages are based on 40″-wide fabric.

Solid colors: 1 fat eighth each of 8 fabrics for foreground blocks

Low-volume fabrics: 4½″ square of each of 16 fabrics for the ghost blocks

TIP *If you'd rather use a lighter version of the foreground colors for your ghost blocks, you'll only need 8 low-volume fabrics. In the cutting section, when cutting the ghost block fabrics, you'll need to cut 2 squares 4½″ × 4½″ from each fabric.*

Ghost blocks in color rather than black and white

White solid: ⅝ yard for background

Backing: 1 yard

Batting: 32½″ × 32½″

Binding: ⅜ yard

Designed, pieced, and quilted by Sylvia Schaefer

Homeward Bound

Finished block size: 3″ × 1½″ • Finished quilt size: 24½″ × 24½″

Flying Geese make up this mini quilt. You have many options for the ghost blocks, but use a solid or very subtle background fabric to keep them well defined.

CUTTING

Solid Colors

Cut 2 squares 4½″ × 4½″ from each fabric.

Low-Volume Fabrics

Cut 1 square 4½″ × 4½″ from each fabric.

White Solid

Cut 8 strips 2½″ × width of fabric (WOF); subcut into 128 squares 2½″ × 2½″.

Note: I like to make my Flying Geese oversized and trim them down for best accuracy, but if you are proficient with the four-at-a-time Flying Geese method, you can make them the exact size. For the exact size, cut your large squares 4¼″ and your small background squares 2⅜″.

CONSTRUCTION

Flying Geese

1. Mark a diagonal line across the wrong side of the 2½″ background squares. Place 2 squares on opposite corners of a 4½″ square of background fabric, right sides together.

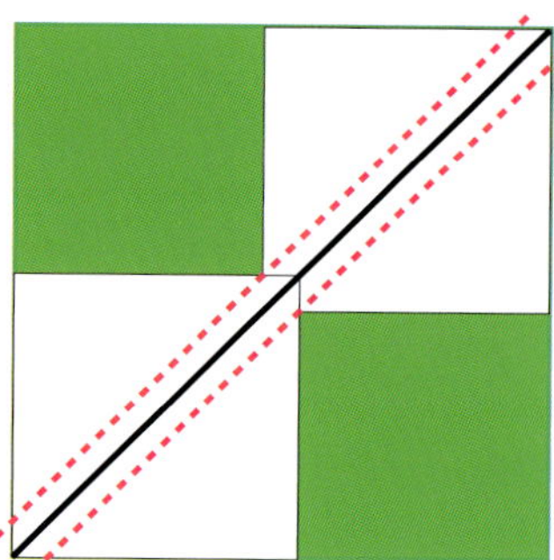

2. Sew a scant ¼″ seam on either side of the marked line (dashed lines). Cut on the marked (solid) line and press the seam toward the smaller triangles.

3. Place another 2½″ background square on the exposed corner of the unit, right sides together. Sew a scant ¼″ seam on either side of the marked line.

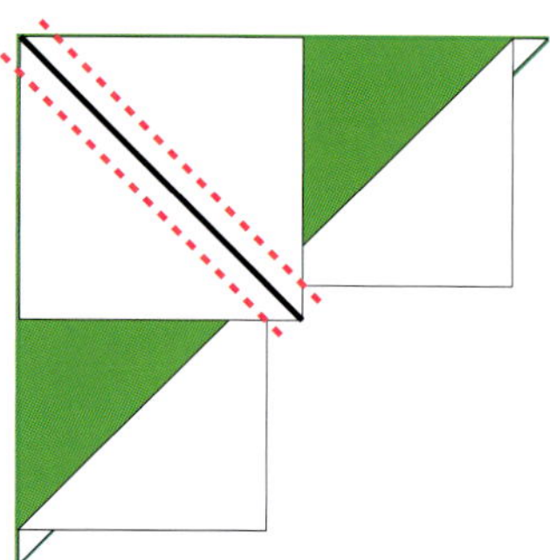

4. Cut on the marked line and press the seams toward the smaller triangle to create Flying Geese units.

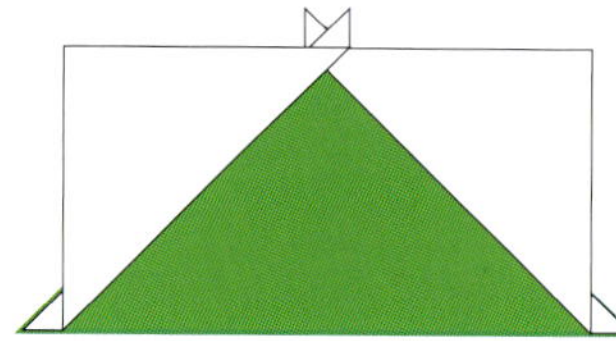

5. Repeat Steps 3–4 for the remaining unit.

6. Trim to 3½″ × 2″, removing the dog-ears and making sure that there is ¼″ seam allowance between the point and edge of the Flying Geese block.

7. Repeat Steps 1–6 to make a total of:

64 ghost units

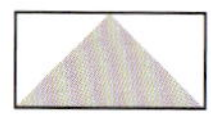

8 units of each solid foreground color (64 total)

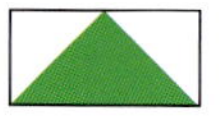
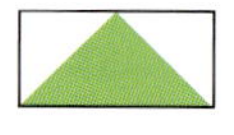
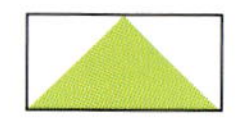
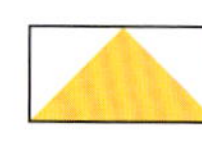

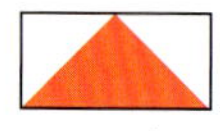
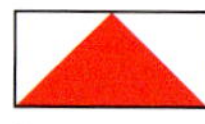

Make 8 Flying Geese blocks in each solid foreground color.

Quilt Assembly

1. Following the assembly diagram, assemble the Flying Geese into columns.

2. Sew the columns together, nesting seams. Press the column seams open to reduce bulk.

Quilt assembly: Arrows indicate pressing direction.

FINISHING

1. Sandwich and quilt as desired.

2. Cut 3 binding strips 2″ × WOF (or up to 2½″, as you prefer) from the binding fabric and piece them together with diagonal seams. Press in half lengthwise and finish the quilt with a double-fold binding.

The sample was quilted with vertical straight lines.

CHAPTER 6

Contrasting Blocks

If you don't want to repeat the foreground blocks in the negative space, an alternative to the ghost blocks discussed in the previous chapter is to use different blocks in the negative space. These can be consistent throughout the negative space or can be a mix of blocks.

CHOOSING A CONTRASTING BLOCK

Thematically Similar Blocks

Using negative-space blocks that differ from the foreground works best when the two blocks have some connection, such as a shape common to both. For example, in this chapter's project, *Where's the Treasure?* (page 62), the blocks in the negative space are Hourglass blocks, which echo the same X shape seen in the foreground blocks. This shape could be considered a contrasting block and a simplified version of the foreground X blocks, so there is some overlap in these concepts!

An alternative version of this chapter's project, featuring Plus blocks instead of Hourglass blocks

Simplified Blocks

Another option that keeps the connection between the foreground and the negative-space blocks intact is to use simplified versions of the foreground blocks. This choice is great when your foreground blocks are complex and could take the form of either a less complex block with the same theme or a block using parts of the foreground block for the negative-space blocks. For example, you could feature a Feathered Star block in the foreground with simpler stars in the negative space. This technique can also be fun for larger-scale appliqué blocks: Choose a smaller block for the background and a scaled-up appliqué for the foreground.

Scrappy simple stars in the background keep the focus on the showpiece center block.

Increased Complexity

Alternatively, if your foreground blocks are on the simpler side, you could experiment with a more complex block for the background. A caveat, though: This choice can make the negative space overly busy, so be very careful about selecting fabrics that are similar in tone and value if the more complex blocks will fill the negative space. Alternatively, you may wish to make only some of the blocks in the negative space more complicated and fill the rest of the space with simpler versions, or even leave some empty space altogether.

This design features solid arcs in the foreground and the full New York Beauty blocks they are based on in the background.

An alternative using only some elements from each New York Beauty block

MIXED BLOCKS

You can also use a variety of blocks in the negative space, which will provide more of a sampler quilt look. In this case, it is less important to maintain a connection between the foreground and the negative space, as sampler quilts are expected to contain a variety of different blocks.

A toned-down sampler quilt makes an interesting background for larger appliqué pieces, such as this Dresden Plate.

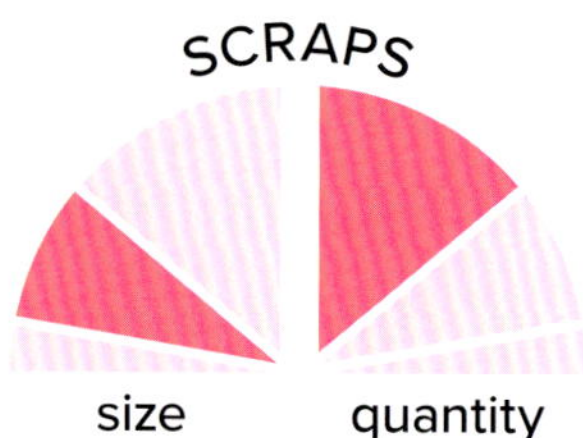

Where's the Treasure?

Finished block size: 6″ • Finished quilt size: 54½″ × 66½″

This quilt uses consistent foreground fabrics, but feel free to make the mint and pink fabrics scrappy as well! To add an extra element of interest to this quilt, pair black and dark gray scraps for the Hourglass blocks and then rotate them carefully to create an extra on-point square effect in the negative space. If you don't like the large focus block, feel free to replace it with more small blocks. You will need an additional 4 large X blocks, 4 Hourglass blocks, and 1 small X block.

Materials

Yardages are based on 40″-wide fabric.

Light pink: 1 fat quarter for giant X block

Pink: ⅝ yard for large X blocks

Mint: ⅜ yard for small X blocks

Assorted grays: scraps equivalent to 2¼ yards for the negative space

Assorted blacks: scraps equivalent to 2½ yards for the negative space

Binding: ⅝ yard

Backing: 3½ yards

Batting: 62½″ × 74½″

Designed and pieced by Sylvia Schaefer, quilted by Sheila Shepherd

Alternative Paper-Piecing Option

If you'd prefer to paper piece the X blocks, you'll find a tutorial on foundation paper piecing and templates linked in Online Resources (page 9).

CUTTING

Light Pink

Cut 2 strips 4¾″ × width of fat quarter; subcut into:

- 1 rectangle 4¾″ × 13¼″ (A)
- 2 squares 4¾″ × 4¾″ (B)

Pink

Cut 10 strips 1⅞″ × WOF; subcut into:

- 26 rectangles 1⅞″ × 7⅝″ (C)
- 52 rectangles 1⅞″ × 3⅜″ (D)

Mint

Cut 5 strips 1⅞″ × WOF; subcut into:

- 19 rectangles 1⅞″ × 4¾″ (E)
- 38 squares 1⅞″ × 1⅞″ (F)

TIP *To maximize the on-point square effect, cut all mint X block backgrounds from the dark gray scraps and all pink X block backgrounds from the black scraps. You can change this mix, but it may affect the overall motif.*

CUTTING continued on next page

Black Scraps

For the Hourglass blocks, cut 23 squares 7½″ × 7½″ (G).

For the large X blocks, cut:

26 squares 5¼″ × 5¼″ (H), cut diagonally twice into quarter triangles

52 squares 2″ × 2″ (I), cut in half diagonally

For the giant X block, cut:

1 square 7¼″ × 7¼″ (J), cut diagonally twice into quarter triangles

2 squares 3⅞″ × 3⅞″ (K), cut in half diagonally

2 rectangles 3½″ × 18½″ (L)

2 rectangles 3½″ × 12½″ (M)

Dark Gray Scraps

For the Hourglass blocks, cut 23 squares 7½″ × 7½″ (G).

For the small X blocks, cut:

19 squares 3¼″ × 3¼″ (N), cut diagonally twice into quarter triangles

38 squares 2″ × 2″ (O), cut in half diagonally

38 rectangles 1½″ × 6½″ (P)

38 rectangles 1½″ × 4½″ (Q)

CONSTRUCTION

Block Assembly

HOURGLASS BLOCKS

1. Draw a diagonal line on the back of a 7½″ G square of dark gray fabric. Pair this with a 7½″ G square of black fabric, right sides together, and sew with a scant ¼″ seam on either side of the drawn line.

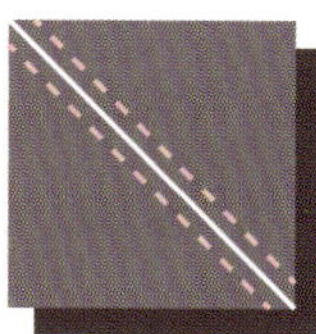

2. Cut along the drawn line and press the seams toward the dark. You will have 2 half-square triangle (HST) blocks.

3. Draw another diagonal line on the back of one of these HSTs, perpendicular to the seam you have already sewn.

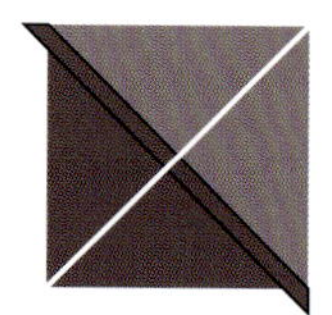

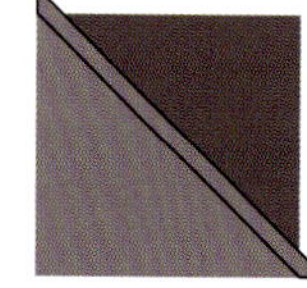

4. Place the 2 HSTs with right sides together, such that the seams nest and the 2 fabrics are not matching. Sew with a scant ¼″ seam on either side of the drawn line.

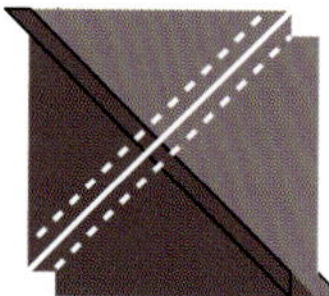

5. Cut along the drawn line and press. You will have 2 Hourglass blocks.

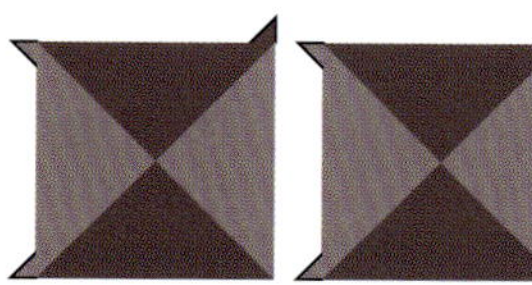

6. Trim the blocks to 6½″ square by aligning the center with the 3¼″ lines on a ruler.

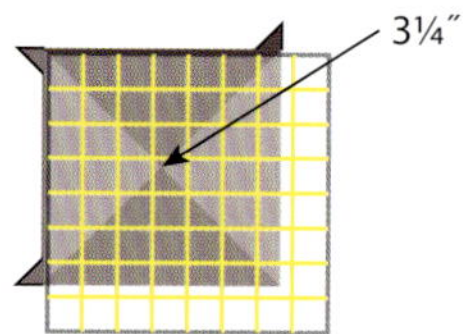

7. Repeat Steps 1–6 with 23 sets of black/dark gray 7½″ squares to make a total of 45 Hourglass blocks (you will have 1 left over).

LARGE X BLOCKS

1. Sew a triangle cut from the 5¼″ × 5¼″ H square to either side of a 1⅞″ × 3⅜″ D rectangle. (The triangle corners will overhang by about ¼″). Press toward the triangles.

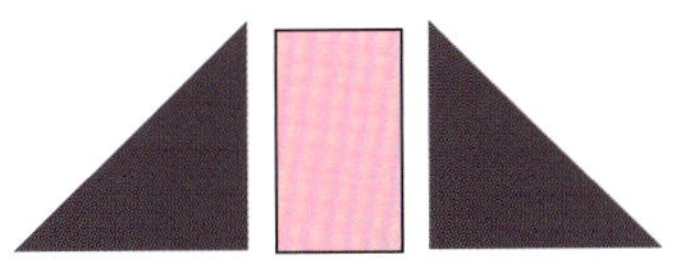

2. Repeat Step 1 to make a second set.

3. Sew the 2 units made in Steps 1–2 to either side of the long 1⅞″ × 7⅝″ C rectangle. Press toward the dark fabric.

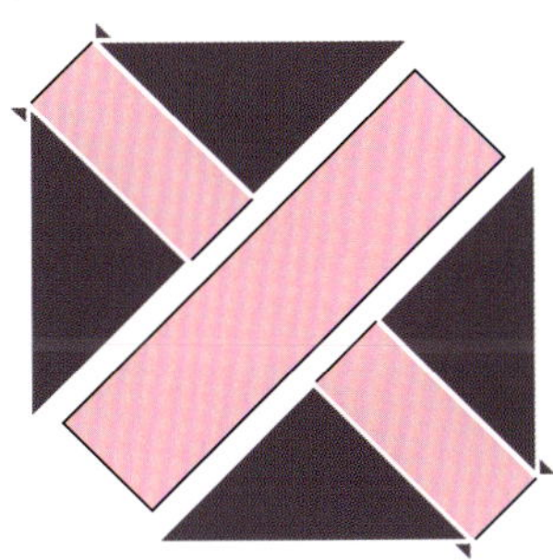

4. Trim the dog-ears.

5. Sew 1 of the small triangles cut from the 2″ × 2″ I squares to each corner of the block.

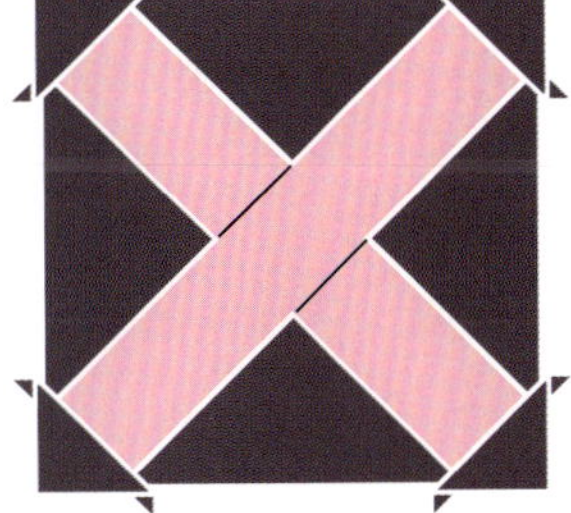

6. Trim the block to 6½″ × 6½″ square, being careful to leave ¼″ between the pink feature fabric and each side of the block.

7. Repeat Steps 1–5 to make a total of 26 large X blocks.

SMALL X BLOCKS

1. Sew a triangle cut from the 3¼″ × 3¼″ N square to either side of a 1⅞″ × 1⅞″ F square. (The triangle corners will overhang by about ¼″.) Press toward the triangles.

2. Repeat Step 1 to make a second set.

3. Sew the 2 units made in Steps 1–2 to either side of the long 1⅞″ × 4¾″ E rectangle. Press toward the dark fabric.

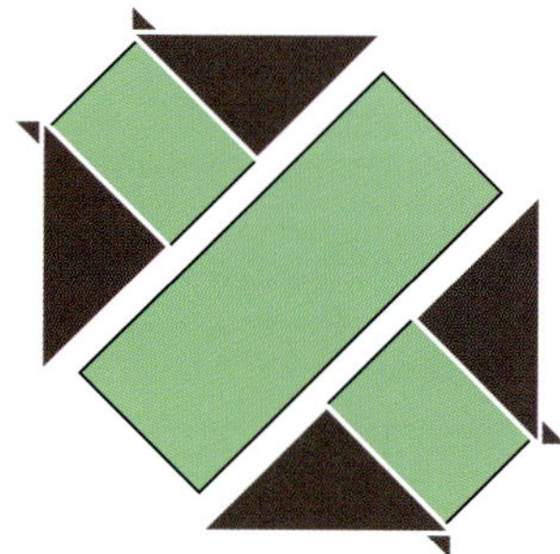

4. Trim the dog-ears.

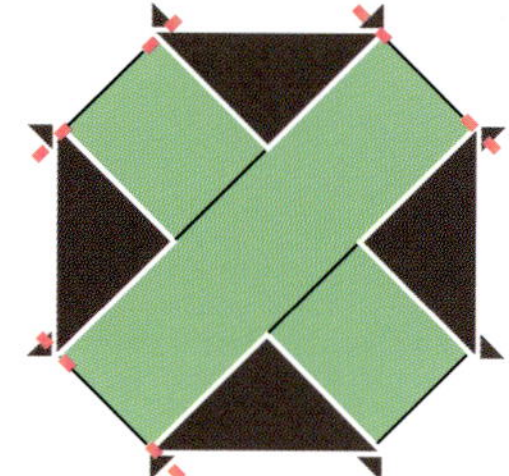

5. Sew 1 of the small triangles cut from the 2″ × 2″ O squares to each corner of the block. Trim the block to 4½″ × 4½″ square, being careful to leave ¼″ between the mint feature fabric and each side of the block.

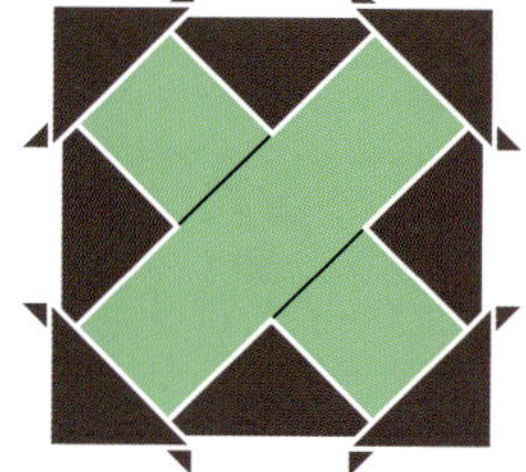

6. To add borders to the block, sew the 1½″ × 4½″ Q rectangles to opposite sides of the block. Press outward and then sew the 1½″ × 6½″ P rectangles to the top and bottom of the block. Press outward.

7. If necessary, trim the block to 6½″ × 6½″ square.

8. Repeat Steps 1–7 to make a total of 19 small X blocks.

GIANT X BLOCK

1. The block assembly for the large focus block is exactly the same as for the small mint blocks, just at a larger scale. Sew a triangle cut from the 7¼″ × 7¼″ J square to either side of a 4¾″ × 4¾″ B square. (The triangle corners will overhang by about ¼″.) Press toward the triangles.

2. Repeat Step 1 to make a second set.

3. Sew the 2 units made in Steps 1–2 to either side of the long 4¾″ × 13¼″ pink rectangle. Press toward the dark fabric.

4. Trim the dog-ears.

5. Sew 1 of the small triangles cut from the 3⅞″ × 3⅞″ K squares to each corner of the block. Trim the block to 12½″ × 12½″ square, being careful to leave ¼″ between the pink feature fabric and each side of the block.

6. To add borders to the block, sew the 3½″ × 12½″ M rectangles to opposite sides of the block. Press outward and then sew the 3½″ × 18½″ L rectangles to the top and bottom of the block. Press outward.

7. If necessary, trim the block to 18½″ × 18½″ square.

Quilt Assembly

1. Following the assembly diagram, sew the blocks together in rows. Note that the Hourglass blocks are turned such that the lighter color always faces the mint blocks, which means that the orientation alternates between rows. For rows 7–9, sew blocks into left and right sections, then join to each side of the Giant X Block.

2. Sew the rows together.

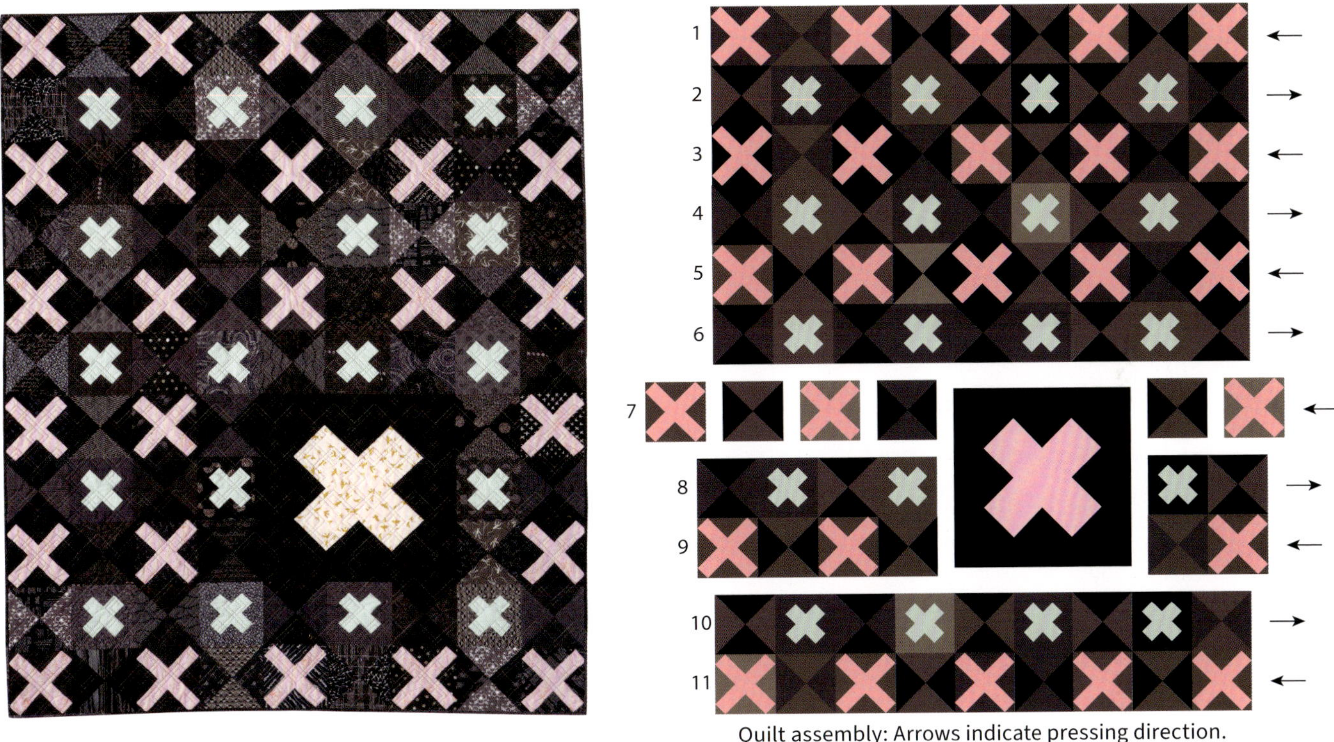

Quilt assembly: Arrows indicate pressing direction.

FINISHING

1. Divide the backing into 2 lengths 62½″ long. Trim selvedges and sew the pieces together along the long side. Trim to 62½″ × 74½″.

2. Layer, baste, and quilt as desired.

3. Cut 7 strips 2″ × WOF (or up to 2½″, as desired) from the binding fabric and piece together with diagonal seams. Press in half lengthwise and finish the quilt with a double-fold binding.

The sample was quilted with the *Exes with Outline* digital pantograph by Barbie Mills of The Quilting Mill.

Improvisational Piecing

The next three chapters include ideas on incorporating improvisational (often shortened to *improv*) piecing. Improv piecing can be defined in a number of ways, but here I use it to mean working without exact measurements or templates. The first two chapters cover **pure improv**, which I am defining as sewing irregular shapes together to create larger sections of fabric. The final chapter in this section covers **structured improv**, which I am using to mean that the shapes and orientations of the fabric pieces are more controlled to create a more structured look, while still not using exact measurements.

In all cases, the colors and fabrics used in the improv-pieced negative space should be controlled. Purists might argue that "true" improv requires randomly selecting the next fabric piece from all available scraps, but this method will create a maximalist quilt. Working without any sort of color plan will most likely not result in effective negative space, and because the focus of this book is on scraps in the negative space, we will leave the subject of maximalism for another time.

CREATING IMPROVISATIONAL FABRIC

1. Find 2 scraps of roughly the same size. If they do not have straight edges, trim at least 1 edge on each scrap straight.

2. Sew the scraps together. It's okay if the ends do not line up.

3. Trim an edge of the sewn-together scraps straight. Feel free to make this cut at a jaunty angle.

4. Add another scrap, trimming an edge straight first, if necessary.

5. Continue in this manner until you have reached the desired size or until you believe that the pieces being added are becoming too large. Once the latter happens, start a new section of improv-pieced fabric.

6. Sew sections of improv piecing together to create larger pieces of fabric.

Variations

Improv piecing has many variations. You can choose one and keep it consistent or mix and match.

Keeping all the angles at 90° is a good choice if your foreground features lots of rectangles and squares and maximizes fabric use.

If you are comfortable with curves, improv curves open up a whole new world of possibilities.

Love traditional blocks but hate matching seams and points? Sneak some wonky traditional blocks into the negative space.

Leftover fabric strips can be sewn together to make a more structured improv block.

CHAPTER 7

Pure Improv Negative Space

Piecing your negative space out of an array of irregular scraps makes an interesting and organic backdrop for your foreground piecing, but it tends to work best when the foreground blocks are also made up of irregular shapes.

FOREGROUND BLOCK CHOICES

You will get the best results if the foreground blocks include some negative space as well so the negative space feels like an integrated part of the design. The negative-space sections within the blocks should also be scrappy so they flow nicely into the surrounding scraps.

It is also helpful if the within-block negative-space sections are irregularly shaped, as this design will help the negative space flow into the odd shapes frequently created by improv piecing. Improv-pieced foreground blocks are a natural choice, of course. Surprisingly, though, because paper-pieced blocks often result in irregular pieces of fabric, they are also perfect for this technique. Additionally, they can provide a nice contrast between the precision of paper piecing and the free-form nature of improv piecing.

The juxtaposition between regular square block sections and improv-pieced sections is a little jarring in this design.

These paper-pieced plants have irregularly shaped negative-space sections, transitioning smoothly into the improv-pieced negative space.

If you do have regular geometric blocks that you'd like to use with an improv background, consider replacing any background sections with small sections of improv piecing—see Chapter 9: Created Fabric (page 88) for more on this technique!

ASSEMBLY OPTIONS

So, what's the best way to put together large swaths of improv-pieced negative space?

The easiest option is to make smaller blocks and put them together in rows and columns, as you would any standard block-based quilt. The advantage of this method, in addition to the ease of handling and assembly (especially when there are square or rectangular foreground blocks to be sewn into the quilt), is that the improv-pieced sections are smaller, so it is easier to incorporate smaller scraps and keep the piecing consistent in scale.

Assembling the negative space in blocks is easiest, but it can be obvious that there is an underlying grid.

The disadvantage of small blocks is that the grid-based assembly seam lines can be obvious. The best way to avoid this look is by making large sections that are not square so long straight seams are angled. This approach also makes it easier to use larger scraps. However, although it can make a fantastic background for large-scale appliqué, this method of construction can be challenging when pieced foreground blocks are involved.

A whole-background approach, where the major assembly lines are at angles, obscures how exactly the quilt was assembled.

One possible compromise is to use an alternate grid. Consider varying the block size, particularly that of the negative-space improv blocks, to help hide the horizontal and vertical seam lines.

Although this design is still constructed with square and rectangular blocks, the variation in size and orientation helps hide the straight seam lines.

If the blocks themselves are not square, you can use this irregularity to your advantage and extend the angled edges to help construct the full quilt. (However, even straight rows of improv-pieced sections can be relatively unobtrusive. For an example of a quilt constructed in this manner, see *I Can't Believe I Have to Say This* (page 16).

This design is assembled in horizontal strips, but the wonky angles help hide the seam lines.

Negative-space improv piecing that is too small

IMPROV PIECING AND SCALE

When considering the interplay between improv-pieced negative space and blocks, it is best to keep the size of the fabric pieces relatively consistent across the foreground and the negative space. A size difference that is too great emphasizes the block boundary, which can be visually distracting.

Negative-space improv piecing that is too big

Negative-space improv piecing that is proportional

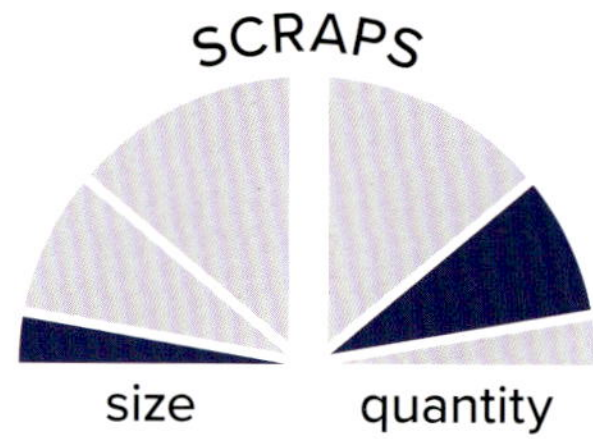

Free-Form Constellation

Finished block size: 6″ • Finished quilt size: 36½″ × 36½″

The layout of blocks here is just a suggestion. If you have a favorite constellation, such as a star sign, that you'd like to represent instead, feel free to adjust the number and position of stars accordingly!

Materials

Yardages are based on 40″-wide fabric.

Assorted yellow and orange scraps: equivalent of ½ yard for stars

Assorted dark blue scraps: equivalent of 2 yards for negative space

Binding: ⅜ yard

Backing: 2½ yards

Batting: 44½″ × 44½″

Designed, pieced, and quilted by Sylvia Schaefer

PREPARATION

Make 12 copies of the Free-Form Constellation A, B, and C paper-piecing templates. If you'd prefer to download and print the templates, go to Online Resources (page 9).

CUTTING

Not all quilters like to precut fabrics for paper piecing, but sizes are provided here for those who do.

Optional Precutting for Star Blocks: Yellow and Orange Scraps

From each scrap, cut the following:

- 3 rectangles 3″ × 2″ (Sections A1, B1, and C1)
- 1 rectangle 4½″ × 6″ (Section A3)

Optional Precutting for Star Blocks: Dark Blue Scraps

For each star block, cut the following:

- 1 rectangle 3½″ × 4½″ (Section A2)
- 2 rectangles 4¼″ × 4¼″ (Sections B2 and C2)
- 2 rectangles 3″ × 4″ (Sections B3 and C3)

CONSTRUCTION

Star Blocks

1. Paper piece Sections A, B, and C for each of the 12 star blocks. Trim the blocks to the outside line. If you need a tutorial on how to paper piece, go to Online Resources (page 9).

2. Join sections A and B and press toward B. Add section C and press toward C.

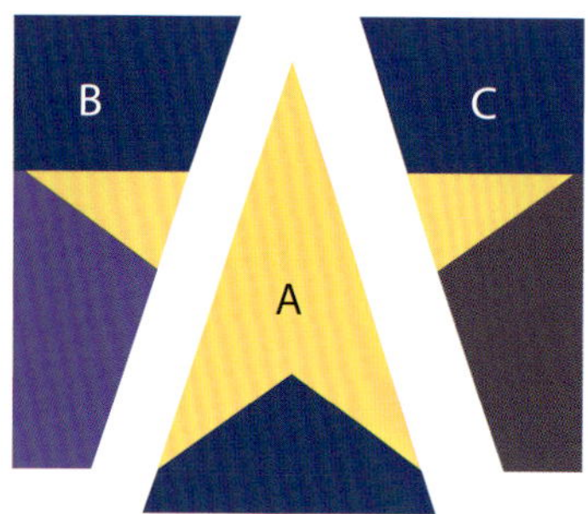

3. Remove the papers.

Improv Blocks

1. Following the improv-piecing directions in Creating Improvisational Fabric (page 68), use the dark blue scraps to piece new fabrics at least 6½″ × 6½″ in size.

2. From these new fabrics, cut 24 blocks 6½″ × 6½″.

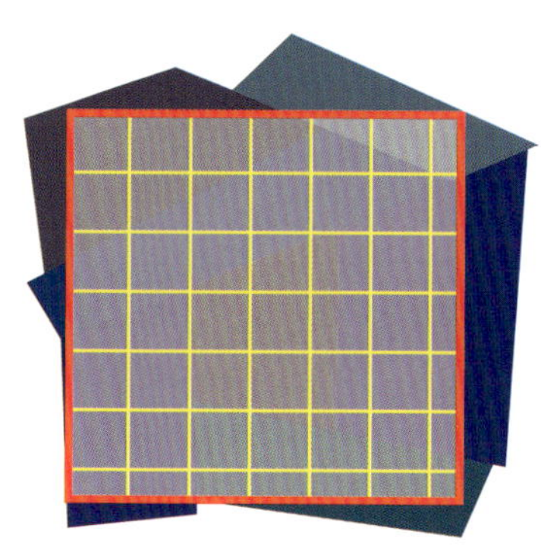

Quilt Assembly

Following the assembly diagram, sew the blocks together in rows, paying careful attention to the orientation of the blocks. Sew the rows together.

Quilt assembly: Arrows indicate pressing direction.

FINISHING

1. Divide the backing into 2 lengths 44½″ long. Trim selvedges and sew the pieces together along the long side. Trim to 44½″ × 44½″.

2. Layer, baste, and quilt as desired.

3. Cut 4 strips 2″ × width of fabric (or up to 2½″, as desired) from the binding fabric and piece together with diagonal seams. Press in half lengthwise and finish the quilt with a double-fold binding.

The sample was quilted with the *West Wind* pantograph by Christy Dillon of My Creative Stitches.

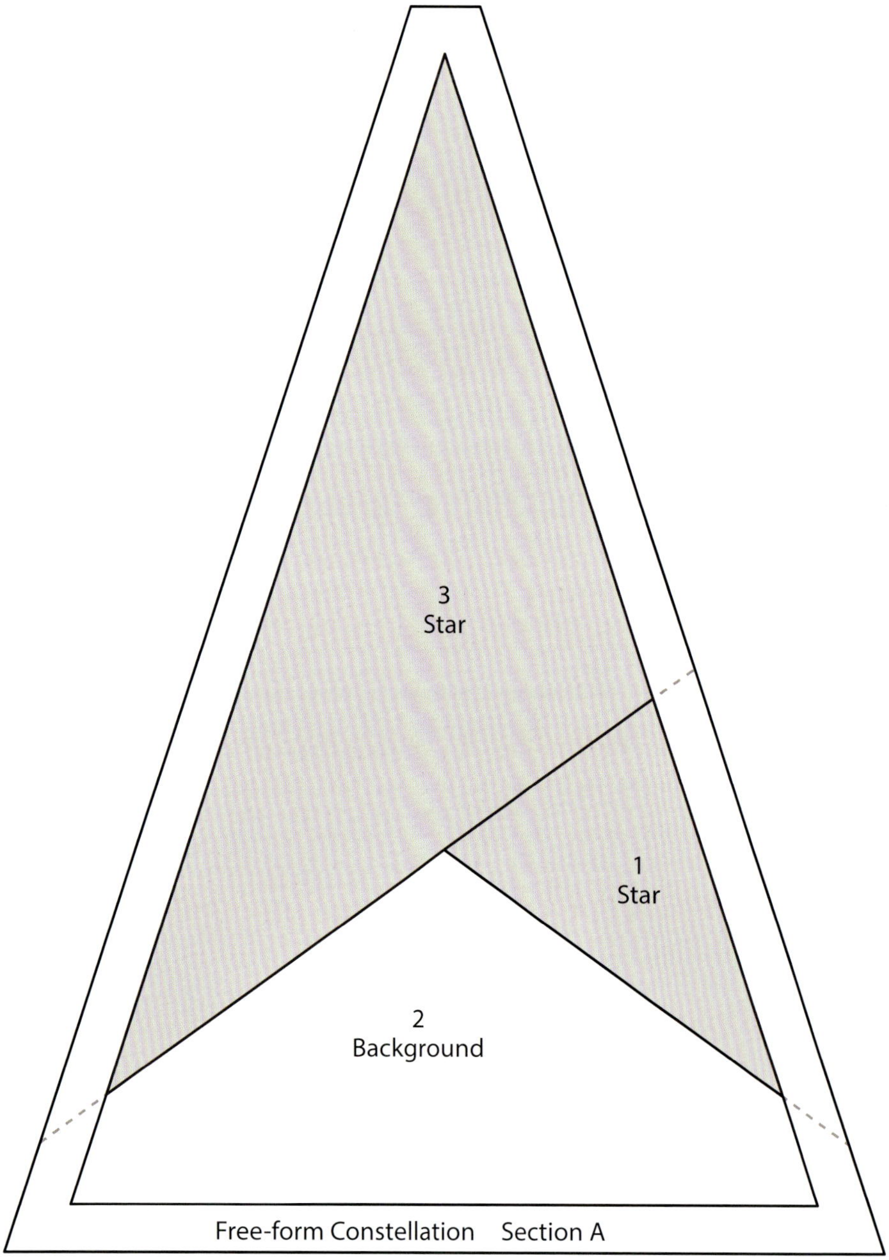

3
Star

1
Star

2
Background

Free-form Constellation Section A

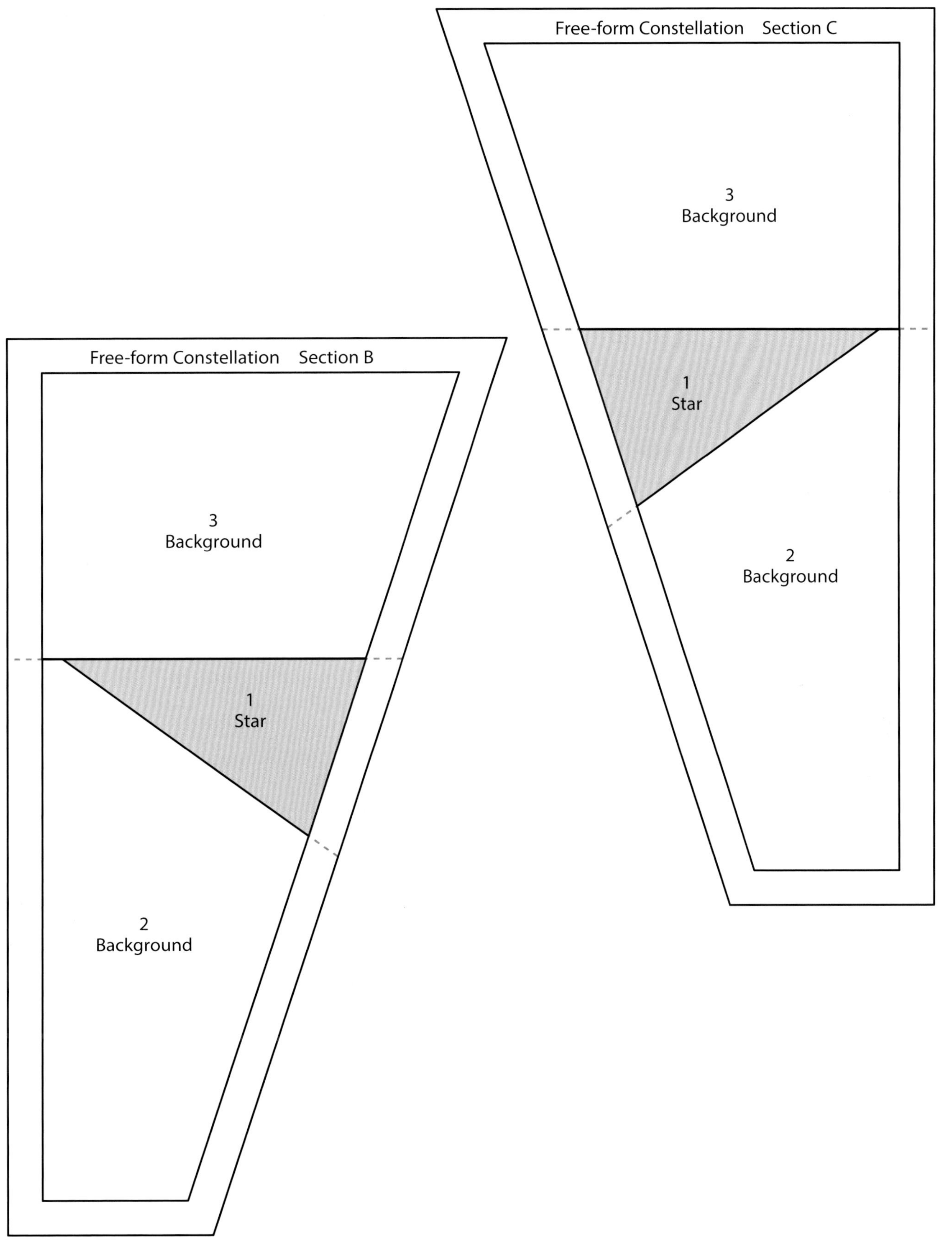
Free-form Constellation Section C
3
Background
1
Star
2
Background
Free-form Constellation Section B
3
Background
1
Star
2
Background

CHAPTER 8

Structured Improv Piecing

Rather than creating a completely free-form fabric, this style of improv piecing preplans the shapes and/or sizes of fabric pieces to create a slightly more structured appearance. Although it can be limited to the negative space, this style of improv is great to choose if the foreground blocks are also improvisationally pieced.

STRIP PIECING

You may already have many strips of fabric in varying sizes left over from past projects. Sewing them together is a quick and easy way to create new panels of fabric from which you can cut multiple blocks. If you do have strips already, straight strips—meaning that the strips are the same width throughout—are easy to handle, and it is simple to keep the panel consistent in width.

You can also use wonky strips to sew panels, where the width tapers from one end of the strip to another. Unless you have pieced in this style before, you probably don't have scraps like this on hand, but they can be quickly cut from wide strips or from large scraps. Using wonky strips furthers the improvisational look of the quilt.

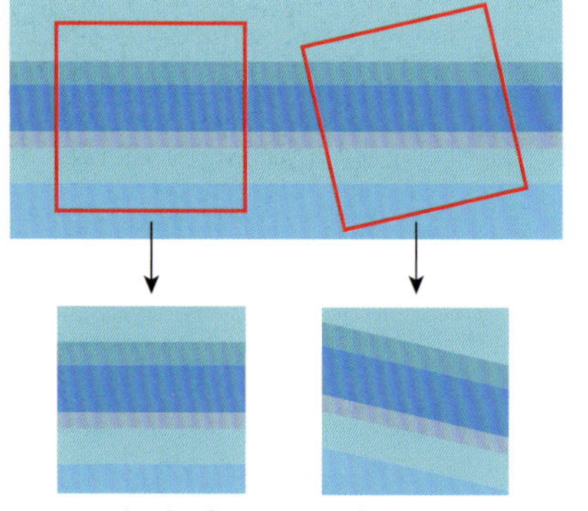

Blocks from straight strips

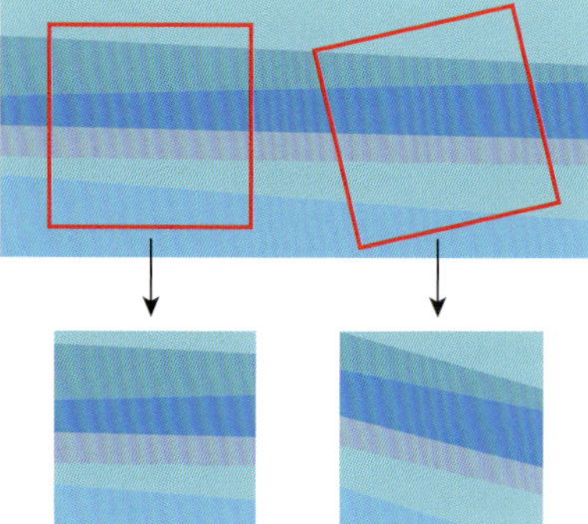

Blocks from wonky strips

Blocks can be cut at any angle (and, of course, you are not limited to square blocks). Varying the angle of strips within a quilt can create interesting effects as well.

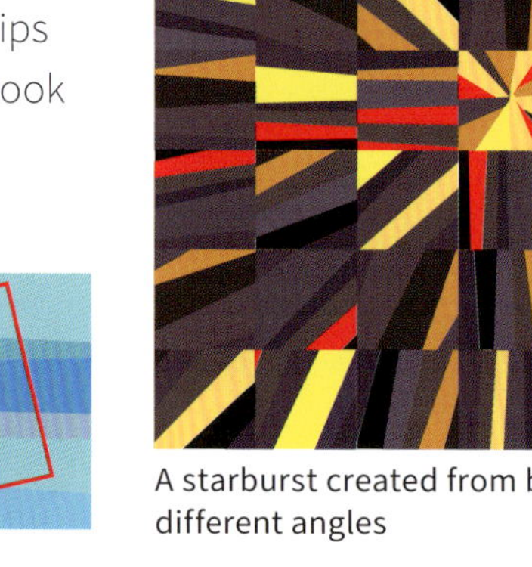

A starburst created from blocks cut at different angles

TIP *If you are a collector of selvedges, consider using them to make an improv-strip quilt! However, keep in mind the need to maintain contrast with any foreground piecing because selvedges are often relatively high in contrast.*

VARYING SCRAP SIZE

Varying the scale of the improv piecing in different parts of the quilt can also create an interesting effect. This look can be achieved with any shape of improv piecing—irregular shapes, strips, rectangles, and more. When gradually increasing or decreasing scrap size, consider combining it with a gradient; see Chapter 10: Foreground Fade-Out (page 104) and Chapter 11: Gradients in the Negative Space (page 114) for more on this idea.

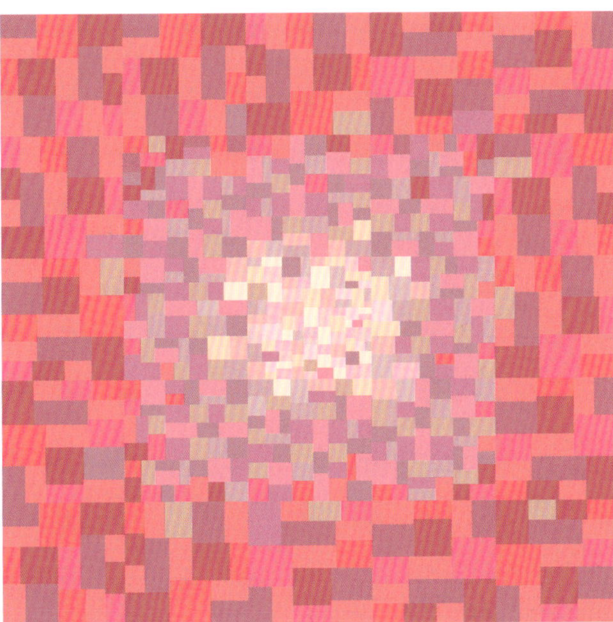

The rectangles are smaller in the interior and larger toward the borders.

TRADITIONAL BLOCKS

Using improvisationally pieced versions of traditional blocks is another twist on structured improv. When doing so, you will want to take into account the same sorts of considerations that you would for regular pieced blocks, so be sure to refer back to Chapters 4–6 (pages 42–67) for more on blocks in the negative space.

An improv version of *Where's the Treasure?* (page 62)

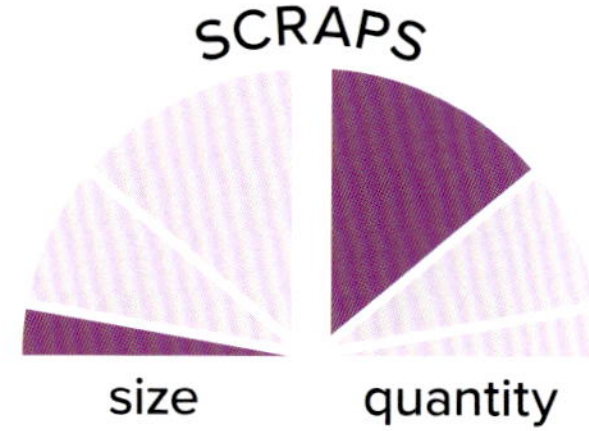

Chain Reaction

Finished block size: 5″
Finished quilt size: 45½″ × 60½″

Leftover strips of fabric are often neglected in favor of more rectangular scraps because the latter are generally easier to use in a block. A project such as this one is a great way to use a bunch of strips—it doesn't even matter whether they're evenly cut!

Materials

Yardages are based on 40″-wide fabric.

Assorted purple scraps: equivalent to 4 yards

Assorted pink scraps: equivalent to 1½ yards

Assorted green scraps: equivalent to ¾ yard

Binding: ½ yard

Backing: 3 yards

Batting: 53½″ × 68½″

Designed and pieced by Sylvia Schaefer, quilted by Sheila Shepherd

CUTTING

From all fabrics, cut strips of varying widths (anywhere between about 1″ and 3″). These strips can be straight (the width is consistent along the whole strip) or wonky (the width tapers from one end of the strip to another).

Straight strip | Wonky strip

Strips should measure between 4″ and 8½″ long in roughly even amounts (however, see Batch Construction of Purple Blocks [page 85] for another construction option). The longer strips will be used in the middle of the blocks, and the shorter strips will be used for the corners.

The number of strips needed will vary, depending on their width.

CONSTRUCTION

Block A

1. Sew strips of purple fabrics together, offsetting them slightly. This offset will vary with the width of the strips; narrow strips should be offset by about ½″, whereas wider strips will be offset by up to 2″. The goal is to create a piece of fabric at least 5½″ × 5½″ in size, with strips running approximately diagonally. Center strips should be a minimum of 8½″ long; use shorter strips for the sides.

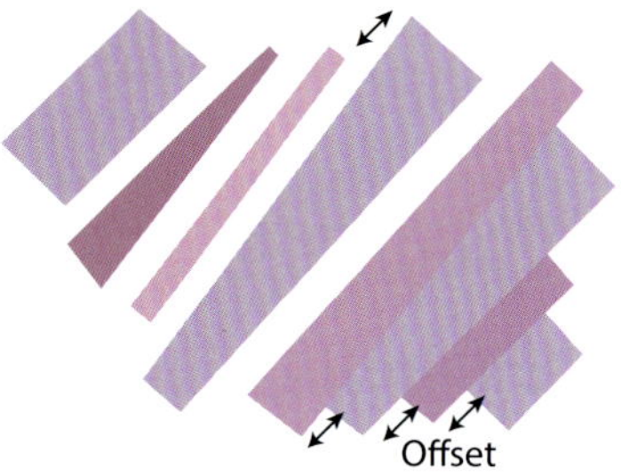

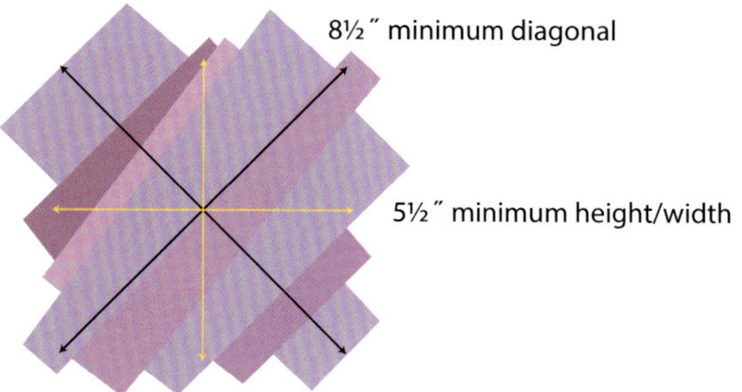

TIP *When sewing wonky strips together, alternate the direction in which the strips taper so that your final construction ends up square-ish.*

2. Trim the completed strip sets to 5½″ × 5½″, with the center strips angled at about 45°.

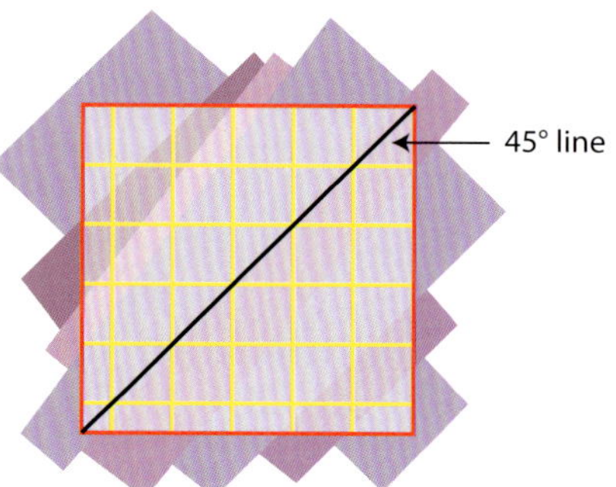

3. Repeat Steps 1–2 to make 60 purple blocks.

TIP *Remove any tiny triangles from the corners after trimming—they will not (or only barely) show after you've sewed the blocks together, only increasing the bulk at block intersections.*

The circled tiny triangle at the corner can be easily removed.

Batch Construction of Purple Blocks

Purple blocks can be constructed and trimmed more efficiently if you construct larger strip sets.

Wider strip sets mean that you can cut multiple blocks from each.

By using strips at least 18″ long, you can fit two blocks side-by-side. Conveniently, this size is about the width of a fat quarter!

With fat quarter or half yard-width strips, three sets of blocks fit, for a total of six blocks from one strip set.

Block B

1. Construct Block B in the same manner, except that half the strip set should be purple and the other half pink.

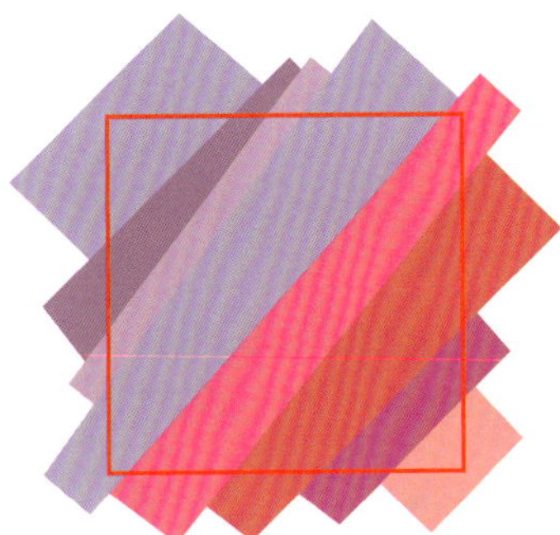

2. Trim the completed strip sets to 5½″ × 5½″.

3. Repeat Steps 1–2 to make 24 purple and pink blocks.

Block C

1. Construct Block C in the same manner, except that half the strip set should be pink and the other half green.

2. Trim the completed strip sets to 5½″ × 5½″.

3. Repeat Steps 1–2 to make 24 pink and green blocks.

Block A
Purple
Make 60.

Block B
Pink/Purple
Make 24.

Block C
Green/Pink
Make 24.

Quilt Assembly

Following the assembly diagram, sew the blocks together in rows, alternating the orientation of the blocks to create diamond shapes. Sew the rows together.

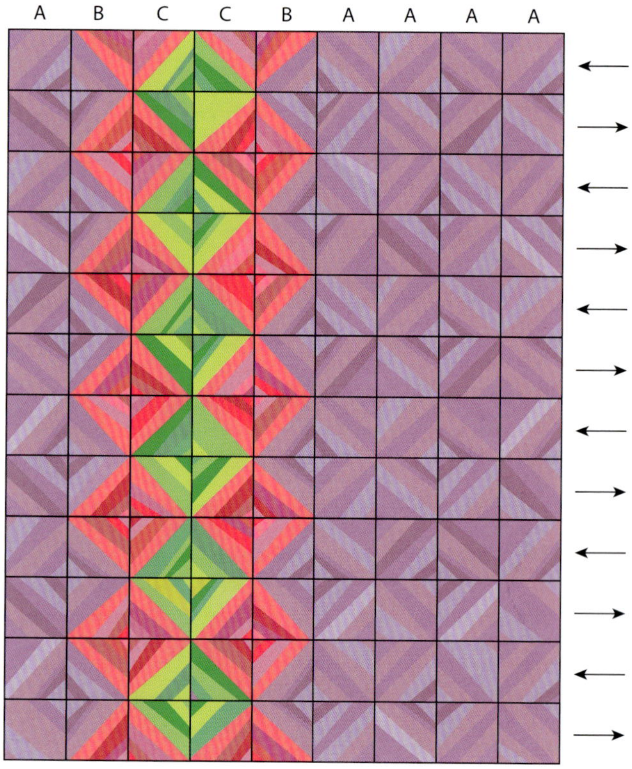

A B C C B A A A A

Quilt assembly: Letters indicate the blocks used in each column. Arrows indicate pressing direction.

FINISHING

1. Divide the backing into 2 lengths 53½″ long. Trim selvedges and sew the pieces together along the long side. Trim to 53½″ × 68½″.

2. Layer, baste, and quilt as desired.

3. Cut 6 strips 2″ × width of fabric (or up to 2½″, as desired) from the binding fabric and piece them together with diagonal seams. Press in half lengthwise and finish the quilt with a double-fold binding.

The sample was quilted with the *Diagonal Improv* digital pantograph by Barbie Mills of The Quilting Mill.

CHAPTER 9

Created Fabric

No matter whether you prefer pure or structured improv (see Chapter 7: Pure Improv Negative Space [page 70] and Chapter 8: Structured Improv Piecing [page 80]), in essence you are sewing scraps together to create new fabric. That "made fabric" can be used as sections of a block, just as you would use any other print or solid in your stash. This "new" fabric can bring a modern punch to more traditional quilt designs, particularly those that feature repeated blocks set across the whole quilt.

Unless your blocks are unusually large, the scale of the improv piecing you use to create this new fabric will need to be relatively small, making this opportunity an excellent way to use your smallest scraps! Perhaps counterintuitively, though, for the improv piecing to be recognizable as such in your blocks, you will need to choose blocks with relatively *large* sections.

In this design, the improv piecing is not evident because the negative space sections are too small.

When the negative space sections are larger, the improv piecing is more visible.

The newly created fabric can be used just for the negative space or for the foreground as well. The latter is an excellent option when the foreground pieces are themselves large. (You could, of course, also use improv piecing just for the foreground and not the negative space!)

Pure improvisational fabric in the negative space of a design

Structured improvisational fabric in the negative space and the foreground of a design

The improv itself can be in either style you prefer. Pure improv provides texture in the piecing. Structured improv can provide more direction and movement: Strip piecing can help direct the eye across your quilt, or it could echo shapes already in your quilt, such as triangles. You can also try incorporating some improv-pieced traditional blocks into your fabric to create another layer of interest.

TIP *When sewing your improv sections, you may want to reduce your stitch length a little, particularly if you will be piecing curves later on, to prevent the edges of your improv sections from coming undone as you handle them.*

Adding a few subtle accents in the form of improv-pieced traditional blocks makes this negative space more interesting.

MORE IDEAS

Another option is to improv piece the blocks themselves rather than using precise measurements. This method creates a more free-form feeling that echoes the improv in the created fabric.

A completely improvisational version of this chapter's pattern quilt, *Peel and Patch* (page 92)

This simplified Mariner's Compass block plays with whether the white shape or the rainbow area is the negative space.

This technique also works well with oversize blocks. For example, you could piece the negative space in an oversize block in a gradient of colors (see also Gradients in the Negative Space [page 114]). Or, you could try simplifying a complex block and filling it with improv piecing!

Rather than being made up of smaller diamonds, this Lone Star's segments have been replaced by improv fabric.

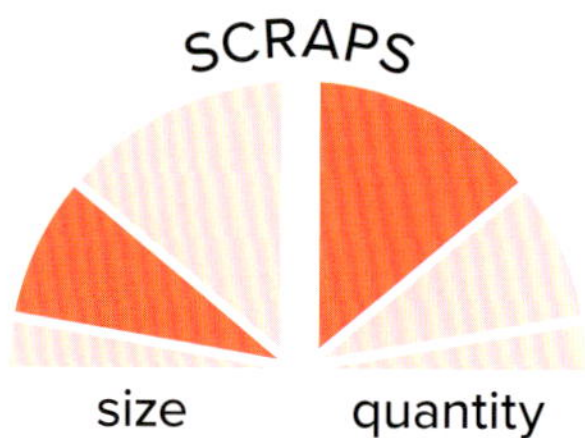

Peel and Patch

Finished block size: 12″ • Finished quilt size: 65½″ × 89½″

This quilt is an excellent long-term project that you can add to as you accumulate scraps of a particular color. Try choosing a color gradient that places the color you have the most scraps of across the middle of the quilt.

Materials

Yardages are based on 40″-wide fabric.

Assorted black scraps: equivalent to 5–6 yards for negative space

Note: The exact amount of fabric needed will vary, depending on scrap size and whether offcuts are reused in other blocks (see Tip [page 94, bottom right]).

Assorted dark blue scraps: equivalent to ¼ yard

Assorted violet scraps: equivalent to ½ yard

Assorted purple scraps: equivalent to ⅝ yard

Assorted dark pink scraps: equivalent to ⅞ yard

Assorted red scraps: equivalent to 1 yard

Assorted red-orange scraps: equivalent to 1¼ yards

Assorted orange scraps: equivalent to 1¼ yards

Assorted yellow-orange scraps: equivalent to 1 yard

Assorted dark yellow scraps: equivalent to ⅞ yard

Assorted bright yellow scraps: equivalent to ⅝ yard

Assorted pale yellow scraps: equivalent to ½ yard

Assorted pale green scraps: equivalent to ¼ yard

Binding: 1 yard for bias binding

Backing: 5½ yards

Batting: 73½″ × 97½″

Recommended: template plastic (13″ × 17″)

Designed and pieced by Sylvia Schaefer, quilted by Sheila Shepherd

PREPARATION

Copy the Peel and Patch templates (page 101) at 200% and trace onto template plastic (if using). Cut out templates. Using a 1⁄16″ hole punch or a large pin, make holes where the alignment dots are. If you'd prefer to download and print these templates rather than trace them, go to Online Resources (page 9).

CONSTRUCTION

Improvisational Piecing

BLACK FABRIC

1. Following the instructions in Creating Improvisational Fabric (page 68), improvisationally piece sections of black fabric measuring at least 13″ × 13″.

2. From these newly created fabrics, cut 35 of Template A. Mark the alignment points on each.

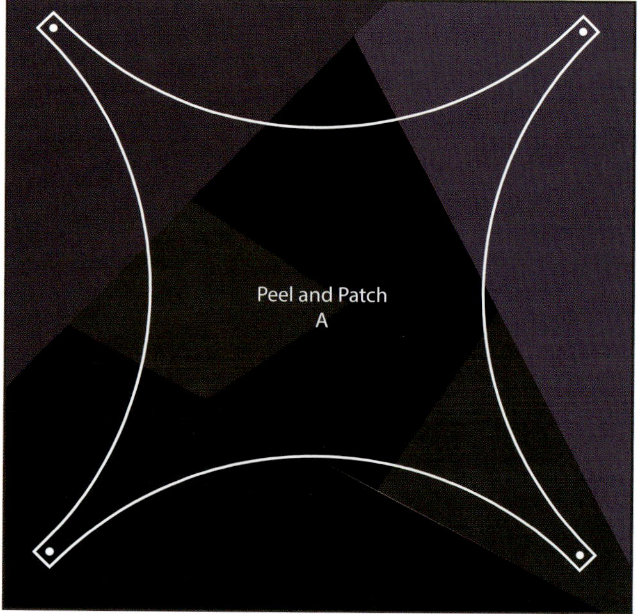

Cutting with Templates

If you are using template plastic for your templates, you can carefully cut around them with a rotary cutter, especially if you have used heavy-duty template plastic. I recommend using a slightly duller blade to reduce the risk of cutting into the template plastic.

You can also trace around the template plastic with a fabric-marking tool and then cut just inside the lines. I like to use Chaco Liners to trace around template plastic and then cut with a rotary cutter and a curved acrylic ruler (which does not have to match the curve precisely; it's just to stabilize the rotary cutter, and you can reposition it as often as you need to). You can also just cut them out with scissors.

TIP: *When cutting your improv-pieced sections down to size, try to avoid getting intersections of pieced fabric too close to the edge of your trimmed pieces, as they can create unnecessary bulk in the seam allowances.*

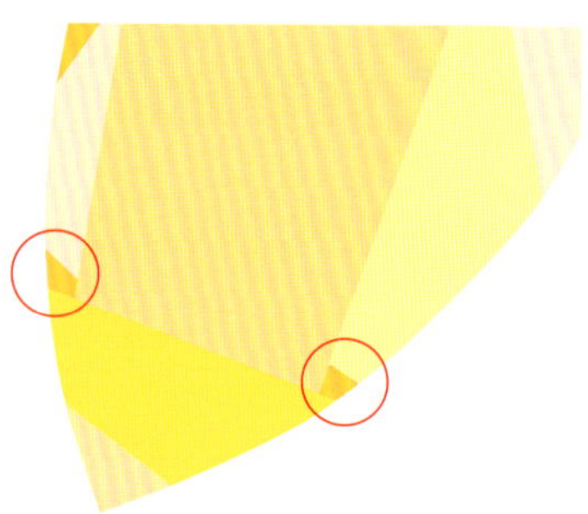

The tiny pieces circled would not, or only barely, be visible once blocks are sewn together.

COLORED FABRICS

1. Improvisationally piece new sections of colored fabric measuring at least 6″ × 13″.

2. From these newly created fabrics, cut the following number of Template B. Mark the alignment points on each.

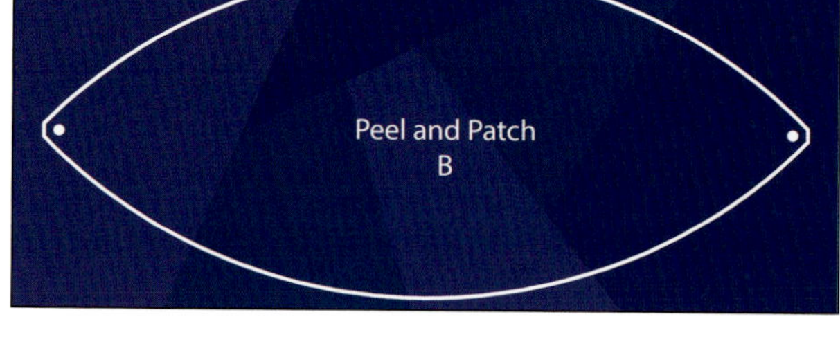

TIP: *You may find it more efficient to improv piece larger pieces of fabric and then cut as many templates as you can fit from each. This method works particularly well for the smaller colored fabric sections. In addition, especially for the black blocks, you can reuse the offcuts after trimming one block to start another.*

Quilt Assembly

CURVED PIECING

1. Pair a Template A piece and a Template B piece. Pin them together at the central alignment point. (You can also find this point by folding the pieces in half and pressing lightly with an iron.)

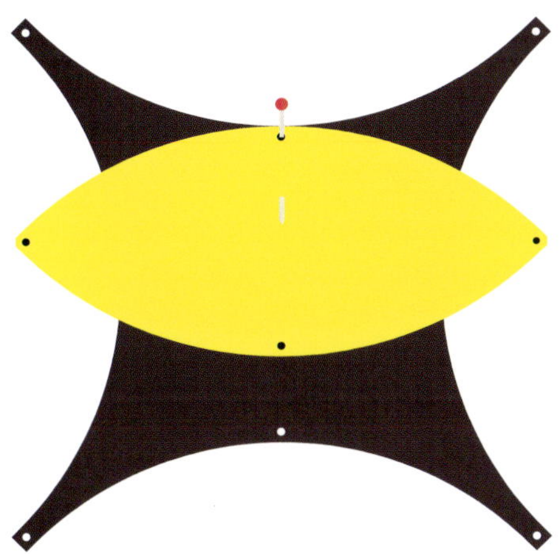

2. With the Template A piece on top, align the edges of the pieces and, depending on your comfort level with curved sewing, place additional pins.

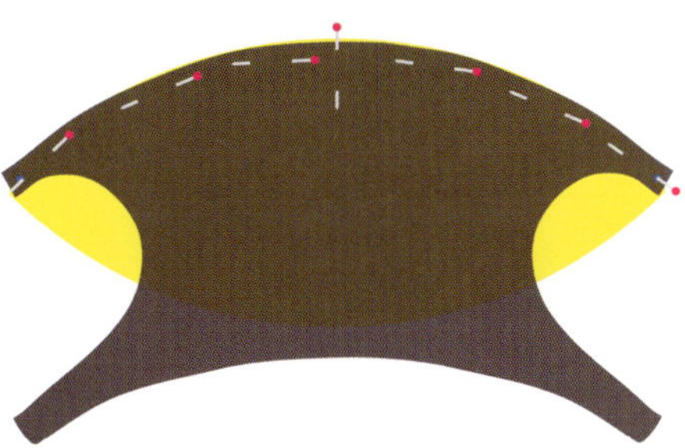

3. With the Template A piece still on top, sew along the edge with a ¼″ seam, starting and ending at the outer alignment dots. Backstitch at both ends to hold the stitches in place. Do not press at this time; waiting makes it easier to attach further sections.

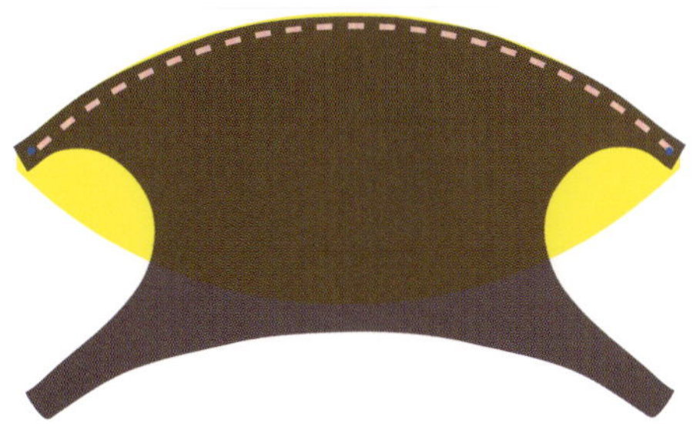

4. Join Template A and B pieces in 7 rows as shown, always sewing with Template A on top. At the points where Template A pieces meet, be sure to fold the previously sewn Template A pieces away from the seam so they are not caught in it.

5. Add Template B sections to the tops and bottoms of the rows as shown in the assembly diagram, again sewing with Template A pieces on top. Continue being careful to fold any other fabrics out of the way of the sections currently being sewn.

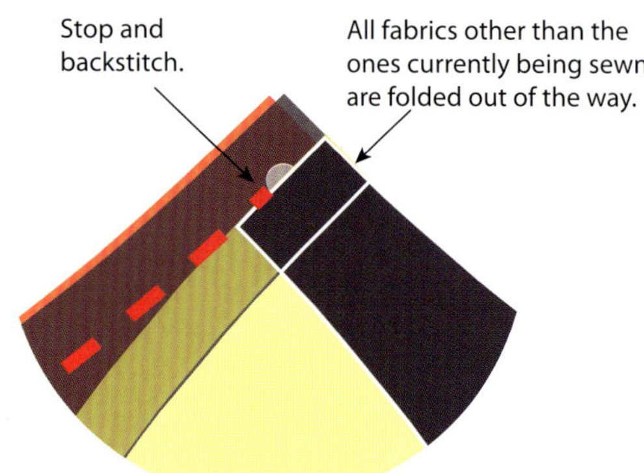

The yellow Template B section is on the bottom, and Template A is on the top.

Quilt assembly: Arrows indicate pressing direction.

6. Press seams on the rows, following the arrows in the assembly diagram.

7. To sew rows together, pin at intersections. Match up alignment dots in the centers of the arcs and pin. Add more pins and then sew each set of rows together with 1 continuous seam.

TIP *You will be sewing some areas together with the concave (Template A) sections on the bottom rather than on top, as is typical with curved piecing. To avoid tucks or other problems, pin those sections in particular very thoroughly.*

FINISHING

1. Divide the backing into 2 lengths 97½″ long. Trim selvedges and sew the pieces together along the long side. Trim to 73½″ × 97½″.

2. Layer, baste, and quilt as desired.

3. Trim the quilt sandwich, cutting carefully around all the scallops.

The sample was quilted with the *Seltzer* digital pantograph by Barbie Mills of The Quilting Mill.

Binding

MAKING BIAS BINDING

1. The edge of this quilt has scallops, so it needs bias binding that can stretch around the curves. To make bias binding, cut a large square of fabric. The size of this square depends on the binding width that you prefer:

Binding Width	Square Size
2″	29″
2¼″	31″
2½″	33″

2. Cut the square in half diagonally.

3. Sew the 2 triangles together along the short sides, allowing dog-ears to overhang by ¼″. Press the seam open.

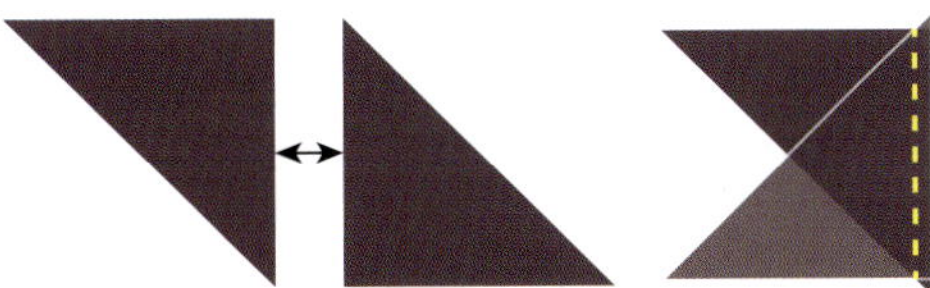

4. Cut binding strips to your preferred width along the long bias edges.

5. Join the strips into one continuous length by sewing them together along the short ends, with dog-ears overhanging by ¼″.

6. Press seams open and trim the dog-ears. Fold the binding in half lengthwise and press.

APPLYING BIAS BINDING

1. Begin sewing the binding along the edge of the quilt on one of the corner blocks, leaving about 6″–8″ unsewn.

2. As you approach an inside corner, stop with the needle down and, using an erasable fabric marker, mark the inside point of the binding by measuring in ¼″ from the edge of the binding and ¼″ down from the next edge of the quilt. Sew to this point and stop with the needle down.

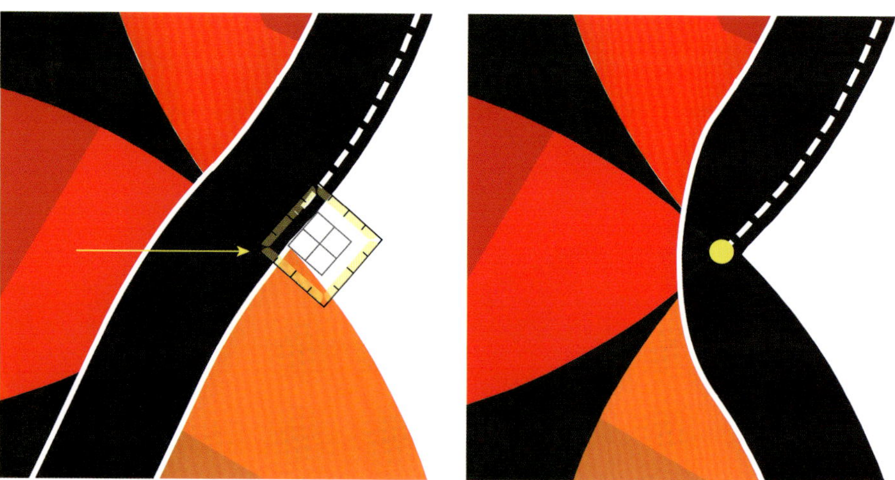

TIP *Lift the presser foot and peer underneath the binding to make sure that the needle has stopped in the right place in relation to the piecing on the top.*

3. Lift the presser foot and pivot the quilt so the edge of the ¼″ foot lines up with the next edge of the quilt. Pull the binding around and lower the presser foot, making sure that the folds are out of the way. A stiletto can be useful here to help manipulate the binding fabric.

4. Continue sewing around the quilt, stopping about 12″ before the beginning of the binding.

5. Joining the binding on a curve works just like joining the binding on a straight edge, except that the ends of the binding should already be cut at the proper angle for a miter. If necessary, trim 1 end so that it lays flat on the quilt and pin it to the quilt.

6. Lay the other binding end (the one with the nice 45° angle) on top, following the curve, and pin it. Mark the end of the top binding on the bottom binding with an erasable fabric pen.

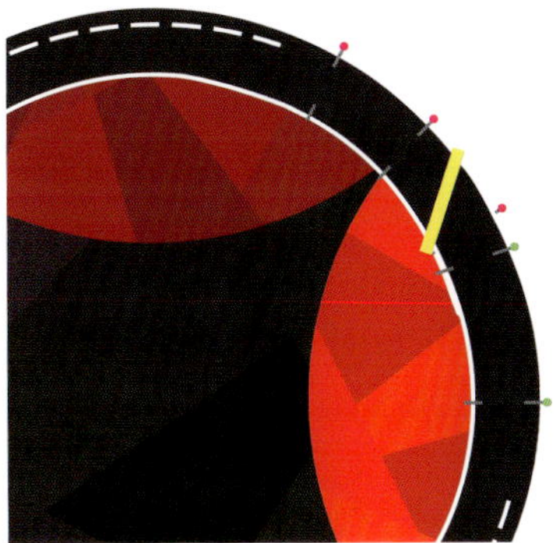

7. Remove the pins and open the binding. Extend the marked line across the whole width of the binding. Mark a second line on the bottom binding, ½″ away from the previous line and closer to the *end* of the binding (red line).

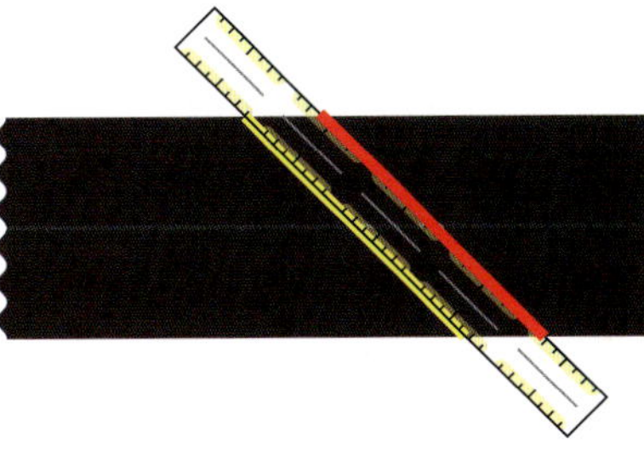

8. With right sides together, line the beginning end of the binding up with the second line. Shift it up to account for the seam allowance.

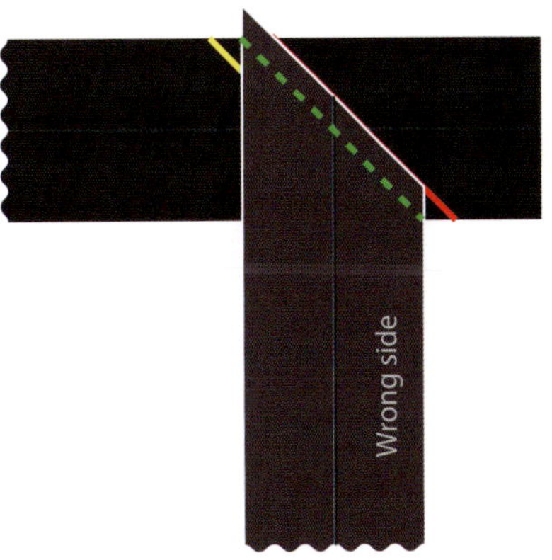

9. Pin and sew ¼″ from the 2 drawn lines (dashed green line).

10. Make sure that the binding fits properly and then trim the excess. Finger-press the seam open and sew this last section of binding to the quilt.

11. Turn the binding to the back and hand stitch down.

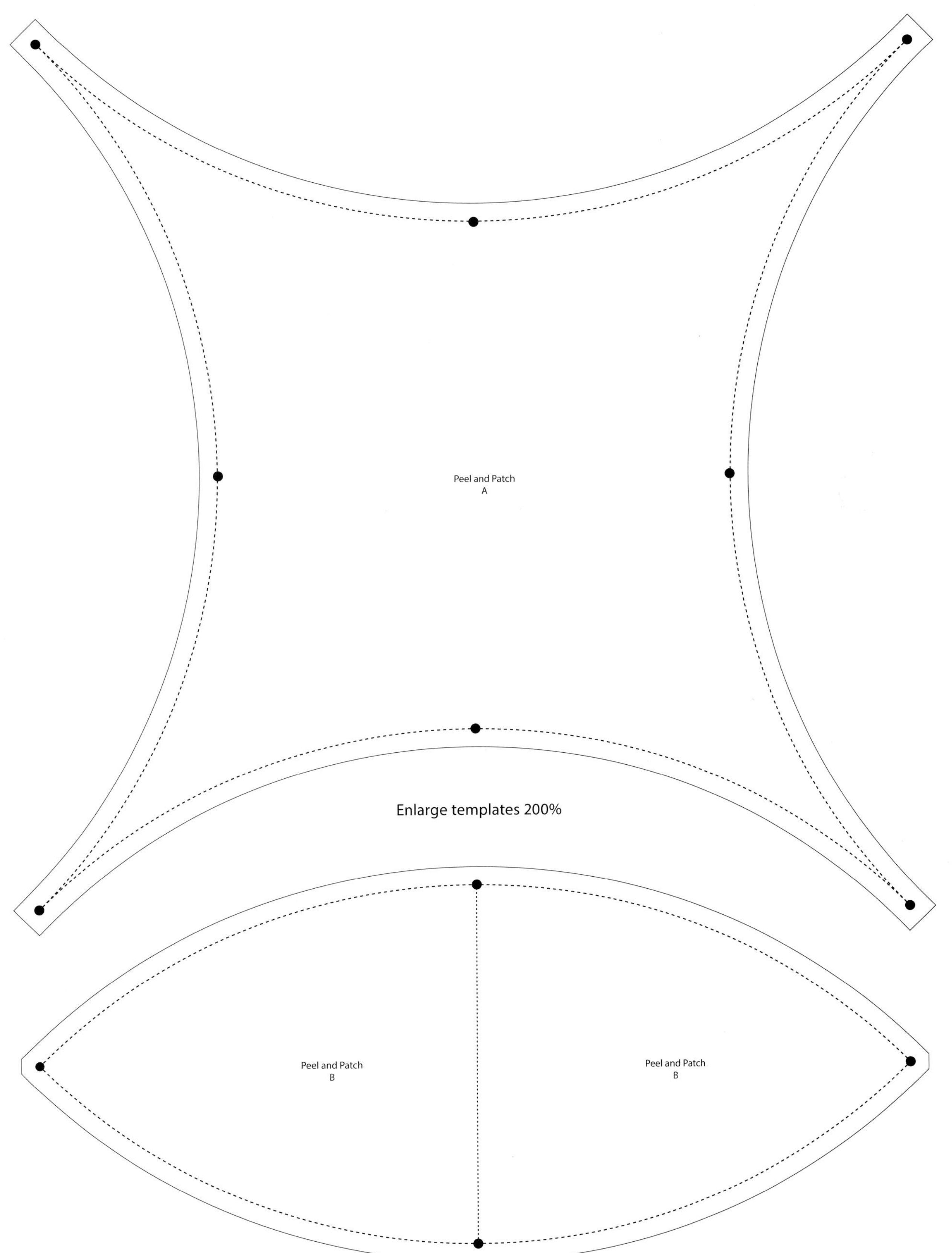
Peel and Patch
A
Enlarge templates 200%
Peel and Patch
B
Peel and Patch
B

Color Gradients

So far, we have mostly stuck with a single color and value (albeit with scrap-generated variation) in the negative space. The next two chapters present more ideas for incorporating multiple colors and values into the negative space of your quilts, specifically in the form of gradients. The ideas in these chapters are intended to combine with the piecing techniques from the previous chapters.

SORTING SCRAPS FOR GRADIENTS

To effectively create gradients from your scraps, you will need to spend some additional time sorting them before beginning your project. Assuming that your scraps are already sorted by color, sort them by value (and/or hue, if your gradient will be between two colors). Aim for three to five piles of fabric here to create your gradient without becoming overwhelmed as to which pile a fabric belongs in. This sorting does not need to be perfect; don't panic if you can't decide, for example, whether a fabric is yellow-orange or light orange! Just put it in a pile. Once your blocks are sewn, you'll be able to arrange them further on your design wall, and you will likely find those transitional fabrics to be very useful.

Sorted blues.

Sorted pinks.

Once you are satisfied with your sorting, start sewing your blocks. A design wall is critical for arranging the blocks and fine-tuning the placement of fabrics, particularly the ones that were difficult to sort. You may want to make a few extra blocks in case you find some fabrics that just don't seem to fit well into the quilt once you have it up on the design wall.

Sorting Fabrics for Multiple Gradients

When sorting fabrics for this type of design, sort the foreground and the negative-space fabrics into equal numbers of piles (again, three to five is a good starting point). Assuming that your gradients go in the same direction, match each foreground fabric pile with a negative-space pile. As you are sewing blocks from each pile, match lighter foreground fabrics with lighter negative-space fabrics. This technique will help you make an extra-smooth gradient when it's time to arrange the blocks on the design wall.

CHAPTER 10

Foreground Fade-Out

Fading out the foreground into the negative space creates an interesting effect where the delineation between the two is not clearly defined, resulting in a dramatic quilt design. Depending on the exact design, this method can also create a three-dimensional or glowing effect in your quilt. Generally, the more blocks in the quilt, the more effective the fade-out effect will be. The blocks can be all the same or a set of related blocks, such as a sampler quilt, but they are best when relatively small and simple.

The fade can go from dark to light, light to dark, or one hue to another. It can also start anywhere you like—try it from the center outward, from the edges inward, from top to bottom, or anything else you can think of. Keep in mind that the viewer's interest will largely be drawn to the area with the most contrast.

An alternative colorway of this chapter's project quilt, *Ombré Symphony* (page 108). With a dark background, the same quilt can fade from light to dark.

Another version of the same design, with hues fading from one into another

ADDING ADDITIONAL INTEREST

A fade-out can make a dramatic quilt on its own, but you may find that your design needs a little something extra.

Accents

Because a fade-out is often monochromatic, it's worth thinking about adding an accent color. This accent color can be all the same, or it can fade with (or opposite from) the rest of the blocks.

Here, the accent reds and yellows fade out with the blues. This design plays with whether the blues are part of the foreground or the negative space!

The accents can also be repeats of the most intense foreground areas, but out of place. Because the fade-out has an element of disintegration or deconstruction built in, it can be interesting to emphasize this look with your color placements.

The accents here are only parts of the pinwheel blocks, creating a sense of disintegration.

You can also try fading out only parts of a block, which will emphasize different parts of the design in different parts of the quilt.

In this design, the on-point squares are much more prominent at the bottom of the quilt because the boxes have been faded out.

Crossfading

A related technique is to crossfade different parts of the block. This method creates an interesting effect where different parts of the block are emphasized as foreground in different areas of the quilt, while the other sections fade into the negative space. This look is particularly effective with blocks that create a secondary design, as you can crossfade the primary and secondary designs.

This block has no built-in negative space, but crossfading allows different sections to act as negative space in different areas of the quilt.

Fading Out Large Blocks

For large blocks, especially those with repeated segments, you may be able to fade out the block itself. This technique generally works best from the center outward, but play around and see what happens!

Note the optical illusion of a glowing background created by the background color's contact with different color intensities in the Lone Star.

The elements in a Giant Dahlia block are not exactly repeated, but they are close enough to work in a fade-out.

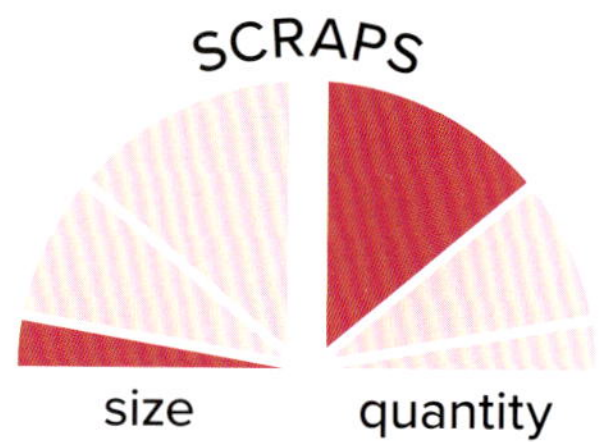

Materials

Yardages are based on 40″-wide fabric.

Assorted dark pink scraps: equivalent to ¼ yard

Assorted medium-dark pink scraps: equivalent to ½ yard

Assorted medium-light pink scraps: equivalent to ¾ yard

Assorted light pink scraps: equivalent to 1½ yards

Assorted low-volume/light gray scraps: equivalent to 2¼ yards

Off-white solid: 3½ yards for background

Binding: ⅝ yard

Backing: 4¼ yards

Batting: 74½″ × 74½″

Optional: Scraps of heavy-duty template plastic

Recommended: 3½″ × 3½″ square ruler

Designed, pieced, and quilted by Sylvia Schaefer

Ombré Symphony

Finished block size: 3″ • Finished quilt size: 66½″ × 66½″

Sort your scraps into 4 piles of pinks for this project.

CUTTING

Photocopy or trace the Ombré Symphony templates, or if you prefer, you can flip to Online Resources (page 9) to download and print the templates.

Using Template Plastic

I like to trace my templates onto heavy-duty template plastic and cut out along the outer line when I have a large number of pieces to cut with a template. It is possible to rotary cut around template plastic, and the heavy-duty kind makes doing so easier. Do be careful when rotary cutting, though, for your sake and for the template's. Sometimes, a slightly duller rotary blade works better so you don't nick the template plastic as easily. (You needed an excuse for having forgotten to change that blade, right?)

Scraps

Cut the following number of Template A pieces from each group of scrap fabrics:

Colors	Pieces	Block
Dark pink	12	Block Z
Medium dark pink	40	Block Y
Medium light pink	68	Block X
Light pink	136	Block W
Low volume	228	Block V

CUTTING continued on next page

Off-White Solid

Cut 31 strips 3¾″ × width of fabric (WOF). Using Template B, subcut into 484 concave curve units, using the cutting diagram to optimize your fabric usage.

Note: You may leave the strips of fabric folded, or even stack 2 or 3, to cut these templates if you are comfortable doing so.

CONSTRUCTION

Block Assembly

1. Pair a Template A piece with a background Template B piece. To sew the 2 together, fold each in half and press lightly with your iron or your finger to mark the center of the curve.

2. Match the 2 center folds up, right sides together and with the Template B (concave) piece on top, and pin them.

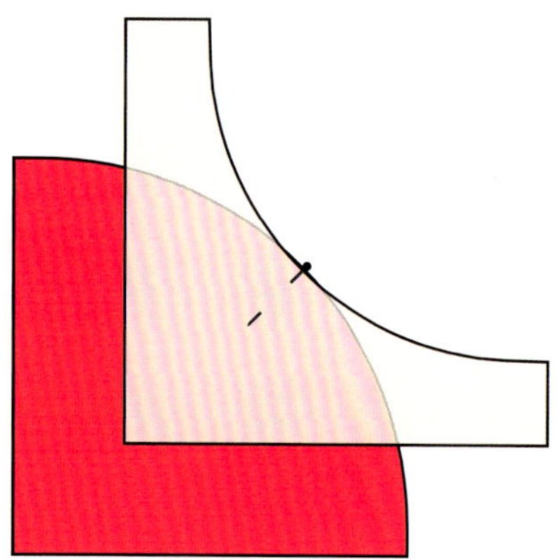

3. Add pins at either end.

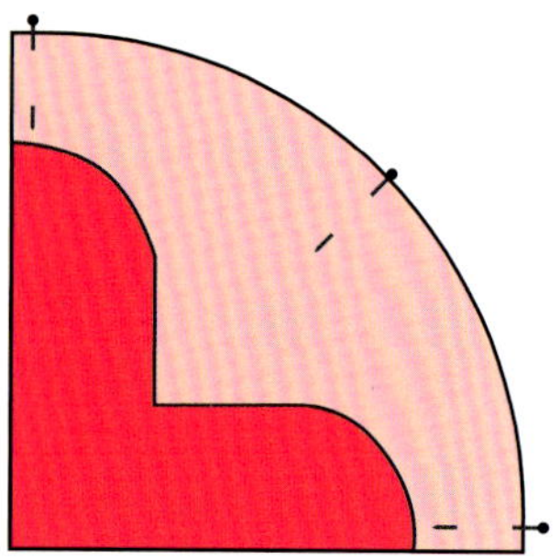

4. Sew along the curve with a ¼″ seam.

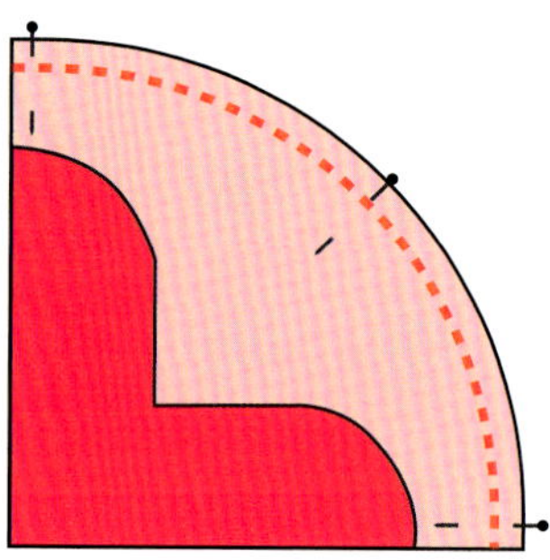

5. Press toward the dark.

6. Trim the block to 3½″ × 3½″, aligning your ruler with the Template A (scrap) fabric. Your seam should be ¼″ from the edges of the ruler.

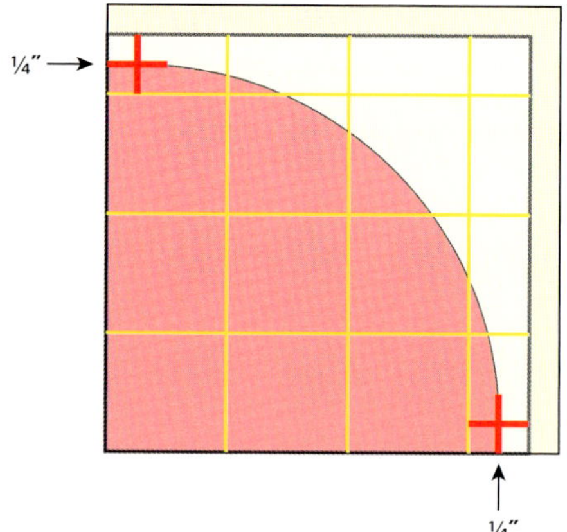

7. Repeat Steps 1–6 to make all the curved blocks.

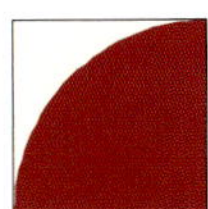

Block Z
Dark pink
Make 12.

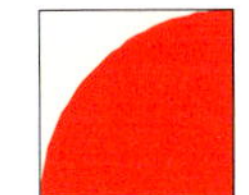

Block Y
Medium-dark pink
Make 40.

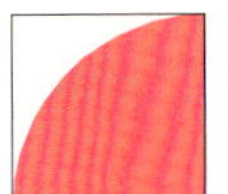

Block X
Medium-light pink
Make 68.

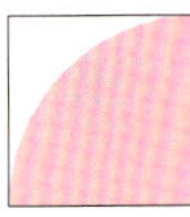

Block W
Light pink
Make 136.

Block V
Low volume
Make 228.

Quilt Assembly

1. Following the assembly diagram, lay your blocks out on a design wall, arranging them to create a smooth gradient.

2. Sew the blocks together in rows, paying careful attention to the orientation of the blocks. Sew the rows together.

	1	2	3	4	5	6	7	8	9	10	11	12	13	14	15	16	17	18	19	20	21	22	
1	V	V	V	V	V	V	V	V	V	V	V	V	V	V	V	V	V	V	V	V	V	V	←
2	V	V	V	V	V	V	V	V	V	V	V	V	V	V	V	V	V	V	V	V	V	V	→
3	V	V	V	V	V	V	V	V	W	W	W	W	W	W	V	V	V	V	V	V	V	V	←
4	V	V	V	V	V	V	W	W	W	W	W	W	W	W	W	W	V	V	V	V	V	V	→
5	V	V	V	V	V	W	W	W	W	W	W	W	W	W	W	W	W	V	V	V	V	V	←
6	V	V	V	V	W	W	W	W	X	X	X	X	X	X	W	W	W	W	V	V	V	V	→
7	V	V	V	W	W	W	W	X	X	X	X	X	X	X	X	W	W	W	W	V	V	V	←
8	V	V	V	W	W	W	X	X	X	Y	Y	Y	Y	X	X	X	W	W	W	V	V	V	→
9	V	V	W	W	W	X	X	X	Y	Y	Y	Y	Y	Y	X	X	X	W	W	W	V	V	←
10	V	V	W	W	W	X	X	Y	Y	Y	Z	Z	Y	Y	Y	X	X	W	W	W	V	V	→
11	V	V	W	W	W	X	X	Y	Y	Z	Z	Z	Z	Y	Y	X	X	W	W	W	V	V	←
12	V	V	W	W	W	X	X	Y	Y	Z	Z	Z	Z	Y	Y	X	X	W	W	W	V	V	→
13	V	V	W	W	W	X	X	Y	Y	Y	Z	Z	Y	Y	Y	X	X	W	W	W	V	V	←
14	V	V	W	W	W	X	X	X	Y	Y	Y	Y	Y	Y	X	X	X	W	W	W	V	V	→
15	V	V	V	W	W	W	X	X	X	Y	Y	Y	Y	X	X	X	W	W	W	V	V	V	←
16	V	V	V	W	W	W	W	X	X	X	X	X	X	X	X	W	W	W	W	V	V	V	→
17	V	V	V	V	W	W	W	W	X	X	X	X	X	X	W	W	W	W	V	V	V	V	←
18	V	V	V	V	V	W	W	W	W	W	W	W	W	W	W	W	W	V	V	V	V	V	→
19	V	V	V	V	V	V	W	W	W	W	W	W	W	W	W	W	V	V	V	V	V	V	←
20	V	V	V	V	V	V	V	V	W	W	W	W	W	W	V	V	V	V	V	V	V	V	→
21	V	V	V	V	V	V	V	V	V	V	V	V	V	V	V	V	V	V	V	V	V	V	←
22	V	V	V	V	V	V	V	V	V	V	V	V	V	V	V	V	V	V	V	V	V	V	→

Quilt assembly: Arrows indicate pressing direction. Numbers indicate the row/column number to aid in assembly.

The sample was quilted with a large walking-foot spiral, starting in the center of the quilt. The thread color was gradually changed from dark pink to cream to match the foreground fabrics.

FINISHING

1. Divide the backing into 2 lengths 74½″ long. Trim selvedges and sew the pieces together along the long side. Trim to 74½″ × 74½″.

2. Layer, baste, and quilt as desired.

3. Cut 7 strips 2″ × WOF (or up to 2½″, as desired) from the binding fabric and piece them together with diagonal seams. Press in half lengthwise and finish the quilt with a double-fold binding.

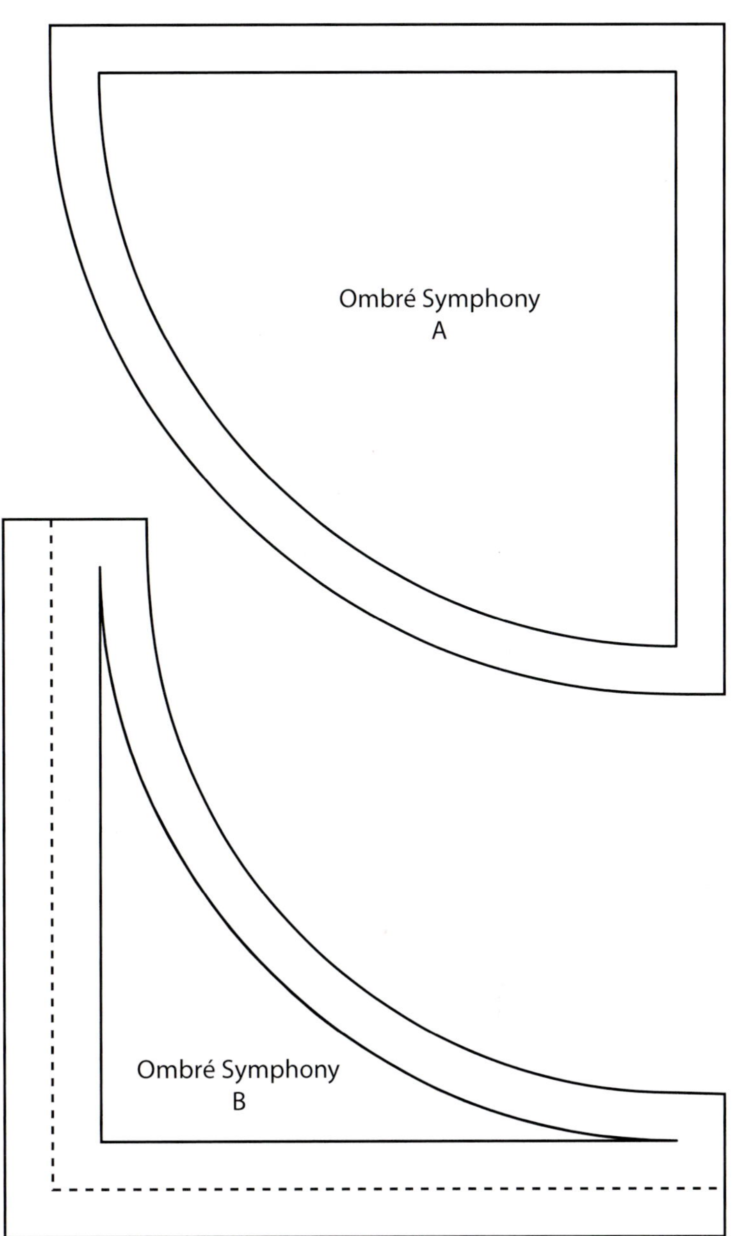
Ombré Symphony
A
Ombré Symphony
B

CHAPTER 11
Gradients in the Negative Space

In contrast to the previous chapter, the gradient can also be located in the negative space rather than in the foreground parts of the blocks. As with fade-out gradients in the foreground, this type of gradient can be from side to side, top to bottom, the center outward, circular, or however you can imagine. Gradients in the negative space work well as a light-to-dark ombré, but you could also create a gradient from one hue to another.

A quilt with a monochrome gradient of ghost blocks in the background

The same quilt, but with a gradient from one hue to an adjacent hue on the color wheel

This technique is also excellent to use when creating a background for a large-scale foreground design, such as a large appliqué.

Large-scale circles on a background of contrasting blocks arranged in a gradient

MULTIPLE GRADIENTS

You can create a dramatic effect by combining a gradient in the negative space with a foreground gradient, as in this chapter's project quilt, *Embers Rising* (page 116). *Embers Rising* actually contains three separate gradients—two gradients of slightly different shades of blue in the negative space (the ghost blocks and the background) and one in the foreground! These gradients can go in the same direction, opposite directions, or completely different directions as the foreground gradient. There are also different color options for the foreground gradient—try the same hue or a contrasting one, or even combine it with fade-out.

This design has gradients in the negative space as well as the foreground that start at the same place but move around the color wheel in opposite directions.

The gradients in the foreground and negative space are the same but go in opposite directions and cross in the middle.

The gradients in the foreground and negative space are perpendicular to one another.

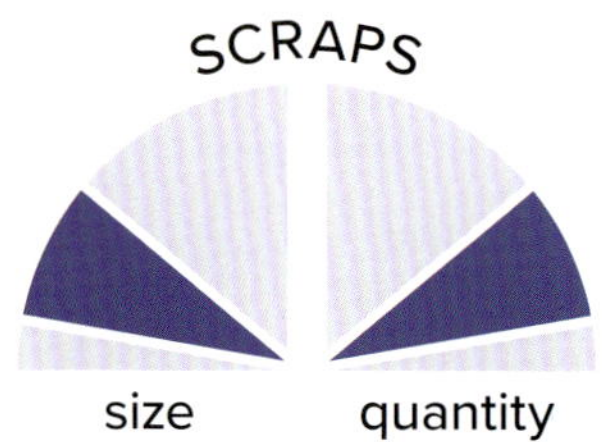

Embers Rising

Finished block size: 3″ × 5″
Finished quilt size: 33½″ × 50½″

For this project, you will need a range of values for the negative space, from light to dark. For the foreground, choose a gradient of adjacent colors.

Materials

Yardages are based on 40″-wide fabric.

FOREGROUND DIAMONDS

For each group, select a range of hues. For yellow, include a few yellow-oranges; for orange, include some dark oranges/red-oranges; and for red, include some dark reds as well as brighter or "true" reds.

Assorted yellow scraps: equivalent to ¼ yard

Assorted orange scraps: equivalent to ⅜ yard

Assorted red scraps: equivalent to ½ yard

NEGATIVE SPACE AND BACKGROUND

Sort your blues into 4 piles, from light to dark. Don't sweat it too much if you are having difficulty deciding which pile a particular blue goes into! It's fine to have a range of shades within each pile; choose your cut-off between each group such that the piles are approximately equal in terms of the number of fabrics in each one.

Assorted light blue scraps: equivalent to ¾ yard

Assorted medium-light blue scraps: equivalent to 1¼ yards

Assorted medium-dark blue scraps: equivalent to 2 yards

Assorted dark blue scraps: equivalent to 1¾ yards

FINISHING

Binding: ½ yard

Backing: 1⅝ yards. *Note:* Assumes 42″-wide fabric

Batting: 41½″ × 58½″

FOUNDATION PAPER

Make 10 copies of Embers Rising Template Y and 105 copies of Embers Rising Template Z on foundation paper.

Designed, pieced, and quilted by Sylvia Schaefer

CUTTING

Yellow

Cut 9 rectangles 3¾″ × 5¾″' for C blocks.

Orange

Cut 20 rectangles 3¾″ × 5¾″ for E blocks.

Red

Cut 23 rectangles 3¾″ × 5¾″ for H blocks.

Cut 2 rectangles 3¼″ × 3¾″ for I blocks.

Light Blue

Cut 26 rectangles 3¾″ × 5¾″ for B blocks.

Cut 5 rectangles 3¼″ × 3¾″ for A blocks.

Medium-Light Blue

Cut 15 rectangles 3¾″ × 5¾″ for D blocks.

Cut 38 pairs (2 each) of rectangles 3″ × 5″ for the background of A, B, and C blocks. Cut in half diagonally, cutting each of the 2 rectangles on the opposite diagonal.

Medium-Dark Blue

Cut 12 rectangles 3¾″ × 5¾″ for G blocks.

Cut 3 rectangles 3¼″ × 3¾″ for F blocks.

Cut 35 pairs (2 each) of rectangles 3″ × 5″ for the background of D and E blocks. Cut in half diagonally, cutting each of the 2 rectangles on the opposite diagonal.

Dark Blue

Cut 38 pairs (2 each) of rectangles 3″ × 5″ for the background of F, G, H, and I blocks. Cut in half diagonally, cutting each of the 2 rectangles on the opposite diagonal.

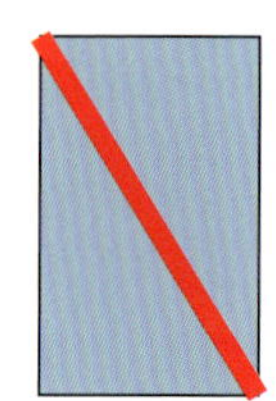
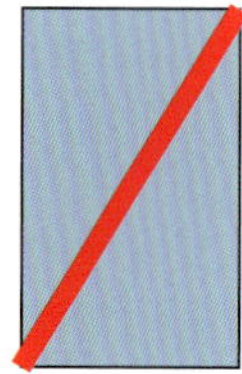

Cutting diagram for background rectangles

CONSTRUCTION

Block Assembly

Paper piece the blocks according to the following table. For a refresher on how to paper piece, check out the Online Resources (page 9) for a link to a tutorial. If you'd rather download and print the templates for this project, you can find a link in the Online Resources section.

	Medium-light blue background	**Medium-dark blue background**	**Dark blue background**
Template Y, half block	Block A • Light blue Make 5.		Block F • Medium-dark blue Make 3.
Template Z, full block	Block B • Light blue Make 26.	Block D • Medium-light blue Make 15.	Block G • Medium-dark blue Make 12.
Template Z, full block	Block C • Yellow Make 9.	Block E • Orange Make 20.	Block H • Red Make 23.
Template Y, half block			Block I • Red Make 2.

The background color (Sections 2–5 on the templates) is indicated at the top. The diamond color (Section 1) is indicated below the block letter.

TIP *Even within your groups, pair the slightly lighter diamonds with slightly lighter background fabrics and the slightly darker diamonds with slightly darker background fabrics. This method will allow you to create an extra-smooth gradient!*

Quilt Assembly

1. Following the assembly diagram, lay out your blocks on a design wall. Rearrange as necessary to create a smooth transition from light to dark.

2. Sew the blocks together in columns, pressing the seams open.

3. Sew the rows together, pressing the seams open.

Quilt assembly

The sample was quilted with zigzag lines, following the piecing.

FINISHING

1. Divide the backing into 2 lengths 41½″ long. Trim selvedges and sew the pieces together along the long side. Trim to 41½″ × 58½″.

2. Layer, baste, and quilt as desired.

3. Cut 5 strips 2″ × width of fabric (or up to 2½″, as desired) from the binding fabric and piece them together with diagonal seams. Press in half lengthwise and finish the quilt with a double-fold binding.

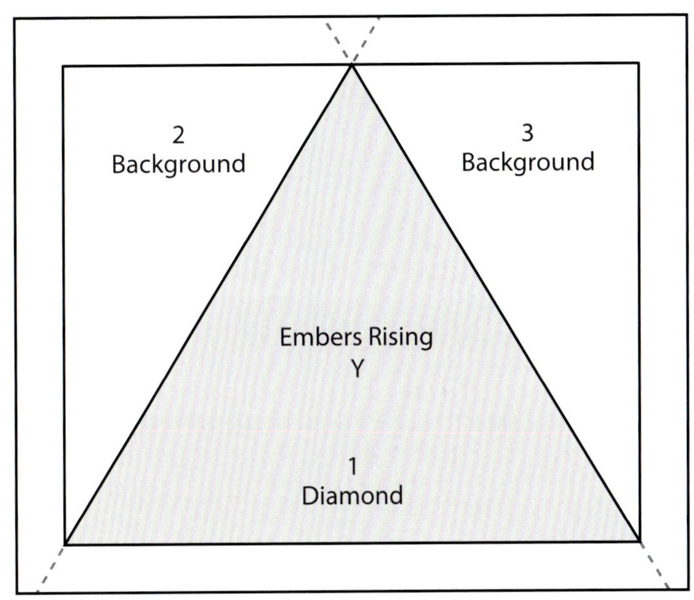
2
Background
3
Background
Embers Rising
Y
1
Diamond

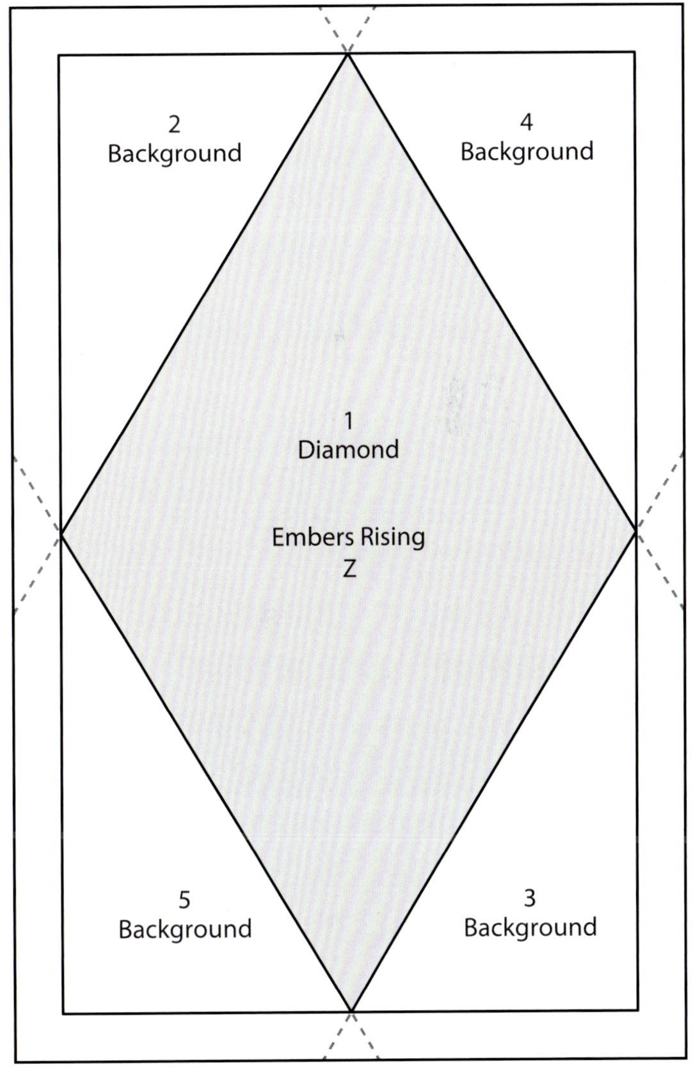
2
Background
4
Background
1
Diamond
Embers Rising
Z
5
Background
3
Background

Finishing Your Scrappy Quilts

Finishing a quilt top doesn't mean that the mission of using your stash has to end too! The backing, binding, and label are all additional opportunities to use scraps and yardage you have on hand.

BACKINGS

Backing Fabric Choices

To use some more fabric, consider making it a "party in the back" and piecing the backing. If reasonably large cuts of fabric are left over from the front, you could include those in the pieced back. The exact definition of "reasonably large" will vary, depending on the size of the quilt and your tolerance for piecing the back after having finally finished your quilt top, but I recommend at least a fat eighth to fat quarter. You can also use cuts of coordinating fabrics. The back is a great place for any multicolored prints that were too busy to include in the quilt top or that include many of the same colors as the top. It's also a great place to use those feature prints that are too pretty to cut up!

You can also include any leftover blocks you might have. Blocks that were rejected from inclusion in the top because they were the wrong size or the fabrics weren't quite right are perfect for the back. Tried out a print that ended up being too busy for the negative space? The block will be just fine on its own in the backing. You might even have some orphan blocks that fit in with the color scheme of the quilt that you could find a home for in the backing.

The backing for *Paradise This Way* (page 24) was made from fat-quarter and half-yard cuts separated by a strip of contrasting fabric for a quick and easy, but still scrappy, backing.

Putting Together a Scrappy Backing

1. To make a basic scrappy backing, gather some large scraps or smaller cuts of fabric that you would like to use. You may want to choose fabrics that fit the color or theme of your quilt top. Include any panels, blocks, or labels to be sewn into the backing. From these, select a few that you are really excited about including.

For *Free-Form Constellation* (page 74), I definitely wanted to use a panel of extra blocks that included the quilt label (written on an extra star block), a strip of gray constellation-themed fabric, and a fat quarter of retro science- and space-themed newspaper ads.

2. Begin by putting your finished quilt top up on the design wall (or down on the floor, as the case may be). Aim for a backing at least 4″ larger than the top on all sides if the quilt will be longarm quilted. For domestic-machine quilting, keeping your backing to no more than approximately 2″ wider than the quilt top on all sides will reduce the risk of getting the backing tucked underneath as you are quilting.

3. Start laying out backing pieces on top of the quilt top, overlapping fabrics generously to account for trimming and seam allowances. Lay the fabrics out so they can be sewn together in horizontal or vertical sections to avoid Y-seams.

My panel of extra blocks was about the same width as the fat quarter, so I added it beneath my fat quarter.

TIP *Choosing multiple fabrics in the same size, such as half-yards or fat quarters, makes putting backings together extra-easy because they are easily seamed and require minimal trimming.*

4. Continue laying out fabric pieces to cover the whole quilt top.

Adding another fat quarter below the panel covered the length of the quilt top, and a full half-yard on the left covered the remaining width, leaving only a small corner at the bottom right.

5. Sew fabric together in groups to create either columns or rows that can then be stitched together. In this case, I sewed the sections together in columns. Trim the edges of the columns or rows straight so they can easily be stitched together.

After a scrap was added to the bottom right, the middle and righthand panels were sewn together.

6. Sew the larger sections together, backstitching at the edges, and then trim the backing to size.

The finished backing, which includes the quilt label. By always laying sections over the finished quilt top, you can make sure that it ends up big enough.

7. As a final step, stitch along the edge of the quilt backing about ⅛″–¼″ from the edge at any spots where you have not backstitched (or the backstitching has been trimmed off) to keep seams from unraveling.

Just a few stitches back and forth over the end of the seam will keep it nice and secure during handling.

More Backing Ideas

When there aren't a lot of scraps left over, try using just a strip of scrappy piecing.

Smaller quilts (about 32″ or less across) can be backed with leftover strips of yardage.

Have some leftover improv piecing or blocks? Incorporate a panel into the backing.

Multiple sections in a gradient of colors go well with a color gradient quilt. Try it wonky or rectangular, as you prefer.

QUILTING

The next step is choosing a quilting design. When the negative space is relatively busy, as a quilt with a lot of scraps in the negative space tends to be, simpler quilting options are often a good choice. Elaborate quilting will not be as visible as it is on a solid or consistent background fabric because the scrappiness draws some of the viewer's attention.

Straight lines, spirals, and all-over quilting designs are great choices that can enhance the quilt while still being relatively quick and easy (and affordable, if you prefer to "quilt by check!"). Most of the quilts in this book were quilted with a walking foot or an all-over design.

If you do prefer custom or heirloom quilting, there are a few considerations. You may want to save it for the foreground, particularly if you have chosen consistent rather than scrappy foreground fabrics, and quilt the negative space with a simpler design. This approach has the added benefit of making the foreground pop a little more. Custom quilting will also be more visible when the fabrics in your quilt are toned down—no black-and-white prints, for example, just soft gray on white prints, and the like. More elaborate quilting can also work when the scraps are large. See *Daisy Flower Garden* (page 34) for an example of custom quilting on a scrappy quilt.

BINDING

A scrappy binding often pairs perfectly with a scrappy quilt. If you have a bin of binding leftovers from previous projects, this is a great opportunity to get rid of a few of those, and they're probably already pressed and ready to be joined together. If your quilt has a gradient in the negative space, like *Embers Rising* (page 116), a scrappy binding is even more effective because you can continue the gradient into the binding without having to worry about precisely matching the binding to seam lines in the quilt.

When you're cutting strips for a scrappy binding, they do not have to be the full width of fabric that regular binding strips usually are; in fact, unless it is a particularly large quilt, shorter pieces will result in a more scrappy appearance. You may also want to try mixing up the direction of the diagonal seams with which you join binding strips.

However, applying such a scrappy binding to a quilt does require a little additional care because there are more seams in the binding. It is best to avoid having seams placed right at the corners of the quilt, where they can make neatly mitering the binding corners difficult. To avoid this issue, lay your binding down onto the trimmed quilt sandwich frequently as you make it to see where seams will fall. Once the binding is completed, it is also helpful to pin or clip it onto the quilt rather than just sewing it off a binding roll to make sure that pieces fall where you want them to.

Binding scraps

TIP *Despite your best attempts at preparation, if you still find that a seam will lie directly on a corner once you are sewing the binding onto the quilt, all is not lost! Stop sewing the binding on, unpick the seam, and then slightly shorten the piece before the corner enough to keep the seam out of the corner. Then, resew the binding seam and continue on your merry way around the quilt.*

Facings

When you don't want to create a small frame around your quilt, an alternative to a binding is a facing. This type of finish involves turning the edge of the quilt to the back to essentially create an invisible finish that will not distract from color gradients or design elements at the edge of the quilt. Many tutorials for this technique are available online, and it's an excellent one to have in your quilting toolbox.

A facing seen from the front and from the back

To see for yourself how I face a quilt, check out my video tutorial at ctpub.com by typing the web address below into your browser window.

tinyurl.com/11606-video

LABELS

Finally, although a quilt label is often an afterthought, it shouldn't be, and it is one last chance to use a scrap or two! If blocks are left over from the quilt top, you could write your information on one of them for a quick but attractive label. Alternatively, a scrap of leftover fabric from the quilt top is a great choice, as long as the print is subtle enough not to interfere with the text.

A label made of leftover blocks from *Ombré Symphony* (page 108)

A label from a scrap matching the quilt top for *Chocolate and Sprinkles* (page 48)

If you are piecing a backing anyway, consider piecing the label directly into the backing, as I show in Putting Together a Scrappy Backing (page 123). The benefit of doing so is that it will be all but impossible to remove, and the chances of a lost quilt making its way back home will be just a little bit better. Piece the label well away from the edge of the backing, though, lest it be cut off when you're trimming the quilt after quilting.

About the Author

Sylvia Schaefer is a pattern designer and award-winning quilter. She holds a PhD in marine science, and her background in science often inspires her quilt designs, directly and indirectly. Her quilts and patterns have been published in magazines online and in print, and her work has been exhibited and won awards regionally and nationally. In 2017, she was awarded the second annual Craftsy Quilt Designer Fellowship, allowing her to start her own line of printed patterns under the brand Flying Parrot Quilts. She has also appeared on camera in *Fresh Quilting* and *Patchwork Nation*. She is an engaging speaker who enjoys teaching and lecturing virtually and in person. She lives in Georgia with her husband, two children, and one flightless cockatiel.

VISIT SYLVIA ONLINE AND FOLLOW ON SOCIAL MEDIA!

Website flyingparrotquilts.com

Instagram @flyingparrotquilts

Pinterest pinterest.com/flyingparrotquilts

YouTube @FlyingParrotQuilts

Facebook facebook.com/FlyingParrotQuilts